Twayne's United States Authors Series

Sylvia E. Bowman, *Editor*

INDIANA UNIVERSITY

William Cullen Bryant

WILLIAM CULLEN BRYANT

by Albert F. McLean, Jr.
Transylvania College

 59

Twayne Publishers, Inc.   ::   New York

MANUFACTURED IN THE UNITED STATES OF AMERICA BY
UNITED PRINTING SERVICES, INC.
NEW HAVEN, CONN.

FOR JEAN

Preface

TO THE EXTENT that any critical or historical study may be considered a ritual act—a serious transmission of meaningful gestures from the past—this book about William Cullen Bryant follows the modes and conventions of the ritual. In this study are a discussion of the biography of the artist, treatment of the poems most generally anthologized, and ideas and information which should be useful for both student and teacher. As much as possible the high spots of previous scholarship about Bryant have found coverage here, but the newer insights of literary criticism and the history of ideas also find their claims duly considered.

But, I would have the reader know, this book aspires to be more than ceremonial—a re-enactment of the past according to established requirements. Like the higher forms of ritual art, this small volume attempts a reconsideration, a reassimilation, and, in a sense, a reliving of the past. My contention is that William Cullen Bryant, as a poet, is far different from the gentlemanly man-of-letters handed down to us by his nineteenth-century admirers. It is time to change the format, to recast our characters, to build anew the sets. For beneath the calm, sonorous surface of his verse lie traces of discord and conflict, a drama of the inner life which has been politely ignored by the critics.

Behind the mask of dignity and confidence, I have sought for the creative consciousness; and, to some extent, I believe that I have discovered it. This is the consciousness that is not satisfied with Sunday-school morality or patriotic clichés but which seeks to draw meaning out of the very jaws of confusion, certainty out of bewilderment, solace from despair. In Bryant's creative process I believe that I have found the deeper pulse of his life and his art. Hopefully my ritual of criticism contains not only what is expected and useful, but also hints and directions for the creative spirits—readers as well as writers—of our day.

A word of caution, however, to readers of this volume: the dynamism of Bryant's creative process manifests itself quite differently from ours. We cannot, with justice, say that Bryant, the genteel patrician, espoused the forms of social protest of our day. Nor can we accuse the respected editor and man-of-affairs of nursing a secret psychosis behind the locked doors of his chamber. Although the problems of life bore heavily upon him, his responses lacked the sensationalism of, say, a Poe or a Whitman. There are few avenues in his work that we can follow toward his personal confrontations with sex, disease, violence, or madness. Even his handling of the theme of death is generalized to the point where the modern sensibility can only reach the lyric impulse with great difficulty. Yet, for all of this, the troubles of life bore heavily upon this man, and he did more than most of us to confront and formulate his problems. The issues are there, and they are our issues as well as his. Within his poetry hope wrestles with experience, the ego contends with its limits in reality, the passing moments of beauty seek to survive in the prosaic passage of time.

It is in the poems themselves that Bryant stands revealed, and it is toward the poems that I have directed the greatest share of attention. Only the initial chapter focuses upon the biographical aspects; only the concluding chapter is concerned with placing Bryant within the context of the American literary tradition as a whole. And the closer look at the poems made possible by this book-length study has brought forth a number of points to confound both Bryant's defenders and his detractors. It has been my position throughout, that the poems should be given every opportunity to speak for themselves; and, only after the most thorough consideration of each work from numerous points of view, have I allowed myself the luxury of judgment. On the whole, it has been the larger picture, the total evaluation which has engaged my thought rather than the passing of specific esthetic judgments. Everywhere that I have searched I have found Bryant the poet—in his bad moments as well as in his good ones—and it has been, for me, an illuminating and rewarding enterprise.

As I review the manuscript in its final stage, echoes of other voices ring in my ear to remind me once more that criticism is not a private ritual. At this point I cannot place all of these voices, much less evaluate their influence. My former teachers, I am sure, will detect the traces of their dedicated work here—as well as the absurdities of which they tried to purge my thought. My associates have also shared with me the production of this work. I would thank particularly the contributors of specific points of information, Sylvan Barnet, Herbert Kleinfield, David E. Philips and Harold Ridlon. Mary Esther Hopkins served well as a research assistant. Charles Holmes, John and Marjorie Harrison, and, most assuredly, Sylvia E. Bowman have provided me with much needed advice concerning style and organization. Acknowledgment is also due to Transylvania College for its contribution, in the forms of released time and funds, to the preparation of this book.

ALBERT F. McLEAN, JR.

Lexington, Kentucky
1963

Contents

Chronology

1794   William Cullen Bryant born November 3, to Dr. Peter Bryant and Sarah Snell Bryant at Cummington, Massachusetts.

1807   Poem published in the Hampshire *Gazette.*

1808   *The Embargo, or Sketches of the Times; A Satire* published as a pamphlet.

1810-   Attended Williams College for one year.
1811

1815   Admitted to the bar after three years of preparation. Composed "To a Waterfowl" and an early draft of "Thanatopsis."

1816-   Practiced law in Great Barrington, Massachusetts.
1825

1817   First important recognition: "Thanatopsis" published in the *North American Review.*

1821   Married Frances Fairchild. Published *Poems;* delivered the Phi Beta Kappa poem at the Harvard College Commencement.

1825   Assumed editorship of the *New York Review.*

1826   Delivered *Lectures on Poetry* to the Athenaeum Society.

1827   Joined the editorial staff of the New York *Evening Post.*

1829   Became part owner and editor-in-chief of the *Evening Post.*

1832   Published *Poems.* Travels through Illinois inspired "The Prairies."

1834   Embarked for Europe for the first time.

1836   *Evening Post* crusades for the right of Abolitionism to be heard.

1842   Published *The Fountain and Other Poems.*

1845 Further travels in Europe.

1846 *The White-Footed Deer and Other Poems* published.

1850 *Letters of a Traveler* published.

1855 *Evening Post* supports Fremont and the Republican party.

1861 *Evening Post* supports Lincoln and the Union cause.

1864 *Thirty Poems* published.

1866 Mrs. Bryant died.

1866- Final voyage to Europe.
1867

1870- Published translations of the *Iliad* and *Odyssey*.
1872

1878 Died on June 12. His estate, estimated at one million
      dollars, was left to his two daughters, Fanny Bryant
      Godwin and Julia Sands Bryant. The *Evening Post* con-
      tinued Bryant's policies under Parke Godwin's leadership.

William Cullen Bryant

CHAPTER 1

A Poet's Life

TO READ THE POETRY of William Cullen Bryant is to engage in an act requiring both historical imagination and perceptive sympathy. If Bryant speaks to the twentieth century, he does so purely on his own terms. Though he created his poetry from the two sources from which all poets work—his heart and his experience—and though his honesty was bountifully rewarded in his own time, he seldom speaks to us of the matters most pertinent to our lives. Neither his remote personality nor his tendentious mind, neither the rural Yankee culture in which he developed nor the momentous national issues which he debated in his maturity seem to be particularly significant when viewed from the perspective of our heavily urbanized, cosmopolitan existence.

To read Bryant in the 1960's is to transcend the limits of contemporary taste and values and to participate vicariously in a creative experiment. To read this poet is to follow the intricate workings of the human imagination—seeking, selecting, contending with its raw materials—in the noble attempt to project a genuinely personal literature appropriate to a free and democratic culture. By restraining for the moment our quarrels with the past, we can possibly achieve some insight into the successes, as well as the failures, of the artistic sensibility as it took root and began to sprout on American soil.

In order to participate in this act of sympathetic understanding, we must discard the critical truisms which have relegated Bryant to the place of a dubious curiosity. The chaste and tidy envelope of the Man of Letters must be opened and its contents put on display. His poetry should be read for its own meaning and beauty without those furtive glances, typical of the academic eye, at the literary giants of other centuries and other cultures. And, in the light of the recent trend of Bryant scholarship, the ideas of the poems should be salvaged from the formalized and over-simplified patterns into which the intellectual historians have categorized them, and then they should be restored to their natural and designated context—the texture of rhythmic and metaphorical language that is the poem itself.

There is no simple method by which Bryant, the poet-at-work, can be resurrected. This study will deal with several facets of the central problem, but it hopefully suggests and anticipates further exploration into the areas of the development of sensibility, theme, voice, and the assimilation of poetic creations by the culture at large. Primary to any understanding of the poems, of course, is an appreciation of the poet's aims, his interests, and his capacities; and it is to this area that attention must first be directed.

I *Major Characteristics*

For some time the major characteristics of Bryant's art have been an open secret. His seriousness, his simplicity, his moralism, his idealism, and his conscious craftsmanship have been the subjects of classroom discussions and scholarly articles for over thirty years. That he shared with the Enlightenment an admiration for the reasoning powers of the human mind and that he deplored both obscurity and emotional extravagances have long been apparent from his poetry and from his critical statements. Equally evident, however, is that he could write of the poet as one who, in the ecstasy of composition, should "Let thine own eyes o'erflow; Let thy lips quiver with the passionate thrill; . . ."[1] And, in poem after poem, Bryant perversely cultivated the qualities of mood in a manner that suggested more the Romantic than the neo-Classical poet. Thus, his profile—as it emerges from sophomore survey courses—is that of a "transitional poet" who somehow could not make up his mind whether to go backward or forward. Any gaps which may have occurred in explaining the man and his works have been conventionally stuffed with the caulking of "Puritanism"—which explains his moralism and his seriousness—and "Nationalism"—sufficient to dispel doubts regarding his social idealism.

These are, of course, all partial truths appropriate to the occasions which called them forth. Bryant's poetry was preponderantly serious, simple, moralistic, idealistic, and skillfully constructed. He was familiar with the neo-Classic temper, having read and composed in that vein during his youth; he responded early and powerfully to the message of the British Romantics; and he later studied German, Spanish, and Portuguese verse. He had been familiar with New England Calvinism in his youth, primarily through his mother's family, the Snells—that long line of worthy and earnest preachers. He had also shown an early interest in politics and, as a young man, become a vocal advocate of democracy and free trade. But all of this is to say merely that he was a clever, conscientious New Englander who, upon arriving in the metropolis of New York City, polished and exploited his talents in the best American fashion.

Nor does Bryant himself do much to correct this image of the successful, self-made poet. The only extant autobiography is fragmentary, breaking off at the very point where the Berkshire boyhood closes and the development of the mature man and artist begins. While this fragment contains hints as to the formation of basic attitudes, its substance is the vivid, charming story of family life in rustic New England. Bryant records the reading of the Bible at home; the stern Calvinism of his grandfather, Squire Snell; and the Federalist enthusiasms of his father, Dr. Peter Bryant. He tells of his own precocity (without any reference to his "genius"), and he also notes that he was, at one point, incapacitated by being kicked in the head by a horse. He remembers the corporal punishment, which supposedly developed the character of the young, and the pictures on the kitchen floor of the folk-lore Satan, "Old Crooktail." With ironic amusement he presents his earliest attempt at rhyming, a versification of the *Book of Job*: "His name was Job, evil he did eschew, To him were born seven sons; three daughters too."

Remarks which strike a somewhat deeper chord, and pertain more directly to the growth of the poet, are those which describe his adverse feelings toward the drunken militia, the quiet shock at his first sight of death at the funeral of a schoolmate, and his thoughtful observation of the religious "awakenings," which had spread—as they did through many rural counties in the early years of the nineteenth century—like an untamable conflagration over Cummington. Bryant recalls, more as observations upon his personal life than as contributing factors toward his poetry, his frequent poor health as a boy, the frustrations which arose from it, and also his early reading in his father's copious library. With half-concealed self-satisfaction, the mature Bryant looks back on his initial publication in the Hampshire *Gazette* of 1804 of a versification of the Hundred and Fourth Psalm, and, in 1809, of the pamphlet sponsored by his father, *The Embargo; Or Sketches of the Times, A Satire; by a Youth of Thirteen.*[2]

In the discussion of his college career, the attributes of character dominate almost entirely over those of sensitivity. In imitation of Sir William Jones, the self-made man whom he had admired in his youth, he extolled industry and fortitude in his remarks on his preparation for college—Greek and Latin under the demanding tutelage of his uncle, the Reverend Dr. Thomas Snell—and the ease with which he—young Bryant—had won recognition for his intellectual abilities at Williams College. Dissatisfied with the low level of instruction at Williams, however, he had made one of those mistakes which the successful man, compulsively it would seem, regrets all his life: he dropped out during his sophomore year and returned home in order to persuade his parents to support him at Yale College. Unable, or perhaps just unwilling, to bear the extra expense of Yale, his family refused to accommodate him. At this point, when he was seventeen, the autobiography makes note of the young man's reading in Southey, Kirke White, Cowper, Blair, and Bishop Porteus; but then it breaks off, leaving his audience to extrapolate, as it were, from the minor achievements to the major ones.[3]

In his eighties, Bryant wrote a poem titled "A Lifetime," in which the chronicle of his life is presented as a series of vignettes.[4] More like the pen-and-ink sketches in a Victorian novel than an honest assessment of times past, the verses describe the boyhood romps in the field; the attentive listening to Bible stories being read aloud in the evening; the young lawyer pleading his case before the bar; the domestic bliss of husband and father; the strenuous labors of the editor; the wanderings of the traveler in foreign lands; and the eventual old man, white-haired and grief-stricken, who stands over the graves of his wife and daughter.

No, William Cullen Bryant was understandably reticent about the creative life which lies buried under these common-places. After all, his struggles with his demon were recorded in his poetry. What the public eye needed, to give balance and justice to the picture, were not meditations on the inward self but the thread by which the common humanity of the poet could be unraveled. These superficial portraits were the clothes in which the naked poet could appear in public, tokens of his respect for the prosaic courses of ordinary lives. Only thus can these trivia be reconciled with the sharp intellect and passionate individualism of Bryant, the poet. For, like the saint, the poet must live two lives: the one by which others know him; the other by which he knows himself.

Bryant's career with the *Evening Post* for fifty-two years, first as an associate editor and subsequently as proprietor and editor-in-chief, provides a notable instance of his willingness to merge into a stereotyped—in this case a corporate—personality. His own account of the critical years of his career was written and published in 1851 under the title of "Reminiscences of the *Evening Post*."[5] Unlike the memoirs of two other publishers, Ben Franklin and Edward Bok, this reminiscence is less concerned with personalities than with policy. As Bryant shapes the image of the *Post* he edited, we identify, to be sure, the man with the institution. The liberal temper—in the style of Cobden and Bright—is Bryant's own political view. The ideological warfare which the *Post* had waged for two decades, and was to continue to wage, on the side of reform, progress, justice, and human freedom, was Bryant's personal war also. Yet the account which Bryant preferred to record was not that of his own contention with men and issues, but the story of the rise of the enlightened and responsible metropolitan dailies.

From Allan Nevins' comprehensive book, *The Evening Post: A Century of Journalism,* comes a sharper picture of Bryant in his editorial role. According to Nevins, Bryant was a bulwark of calm strength and conviction: "The foundation of Bryant's power as an editor lay simply in his soundness of judgment and his unwavering courage in maintaining it."[6] Faced with innumerable issues of every size and dimension—the tariff,

Jackson's attack on the national bank, the Mexican War, imperialism, penal reform, the rights of labor, internal improvements, international copyright, freedom of the press, stabilization of the currency—Bryant and the *Post* maintained a critical alertness and perseverance which commended itself to a large following.

Professor Nevins also makes the point that the *Post* was a paper with principles: "Freedom and democracy—to these two principles every utterance of the *Evening Post* in its fifty years under Bryant was referred. Other journals might think of the day only and let the morrow take care of itself, but he was solicitous that each issue should fit into the exposition of a policy good for the year and the decade."[7] Nevertheless, influential as these principles of freedom and democracy may have been, Bryant and the *Post* carefully refrained from systematically defining them, or from making any broader application of them than the events of the day warranted. As Godwin (associate editor under Bryant and successor to the editorship) has noted, Bryant stopped far short of doctrinaire commitments. His consistency, it would seem, was more pragmatic than absolute. If the fruit of his judgment was freely articulated for public consumption, the roots of his principles remained buried deep within.

Nor does the social image of the man lead us very far into his creative center. His friendships were many and various; but close companions, outside of his family, were rare. His eulogies on Cooper, Irving, and Verplank reveal only a slight personal warmth for these men with whom he had associated; and his poems to William Leggett, John Lothrop Motley, and Thomas Cole[8] were distinguished for their lofty and abstract praise of public virtues. He appears to have lacked that appeal and social charm which were characteristic of many of the nineteenth-century men of letters and to have made little effort to win friends or readers through the application of personal warmth. A magazine writer of the early 1830's expressed a prevailing view of Bryant when he noted that "His manners are quiet and unassuming, and marked with a slight dash of diffidence; and his conversation (when he does converse, for he is more used to thinking than talking), is remarkably free from pretension, and is characterized by good sense rather than genius."[9]

Parke Godwin, associate on the *Post* and the son-in-law and biographer of Bryant, confirms this impression while seeing deeper into the man. Godwin observed that it was the action of the eyes which was the key to his presence and that his voice was his best recommendation in social intercourse. This is how Godwin describes his first meeting with the poet in 1832:

> He was of middle age and medium height, spare in figure, with a clean-shaven face, unusually large head, bright eyes, and a wearied, severe, almost saturnine expression of countenance. One, however, remarked at once the exceeding gentleness of his manner, and a rare sweetness in the tone of his voice, as well as an extraordinary purity in his selection and pronunciation of English. His conversation was easy, but not fluent, and he had the habit of looking the person he addressed so directly in the eyes that it was not a little embarrassing at first. A certain air of abstractedness in his face made you set him down as a scholar whose thoughts were wandering away to his books; and yet the deep lines about the mouth told of struggle either with himself or with the world.[10]

Nearly thirty years later, Nathaniel Hawthorne, who was himself known for his quietness and reserve, was to remark on the qualities of Bryant's eyes, finding them "keen eyes, without much softness in them." And his assessment of his visitor bears out that of Godwin: "[Bryant] was not in the least degree excited about [the suffering of Charles Sumner] or any other subject. He uttered neither passion nor poetry, but excellent good sense, and accurate information, on whatever subject transpired; a very pleasant man to associate with, but rather cold, I should imagine, if one should seek to touch his heart with one's own. He shook hands kindly all round, but not with any warmth of gripe [sic], although the ease of his deportment had put all on sociable terms with him."[11]

Perhaps this remoteness in Bryant's bearing is responsible for the scarcity of friendly comment by his contemporaries upon his art. Certainly his personal correspondence, even with his intimates, supplies little insight into his working methods or his creative goals. When Bryant corresponded about his poetry, his remarks pertained almost exclusively to publication and to critical response. Even toward Edward T. Channing, who, as an editor of the *North American Review*, bore a major responsibility for Bryant's emergence as a national poet, he could maintain a cool distance and a relationship entirely devoid of any but the most prosaic of considerations. In 1819, upon being strenuously pressed by Channing for more material, Bryant replied with a diffidence that is a mixture of modesty and archness: "I may perhaps, some time or other, venture a little collection in print—for I do not write much—and should it be favorably received—it may give me more courage to do something more."[12]

Collect them he did, two years later in *Poems*, and roughly each decade throughout his life. *Poems* was updated in 1832, *The Fountain and Other Poems* appeared in 1842, and then followed *The White-Footed Deer and Other Poems* (1846), *Thirty Poems* (1864), and, finally, a nearly complete collection two years before his death, *The Poetical Works of William Cullen Bryant* (1876). Yet lacking in all of these collections is a formulated intention or principle of selection. Bryant gave his readers no caption (nor useful introduction) to lead into the heart of his verse, such as we find, of course, in *Leaves of Grass, Children of the Night,* and *North of Boston.* Cast like commodities upon the market, it is not surprising that Bryant's poems should be accepted as the products of an entirely reputable but unknowable manufacturer.

In "The Poet" Bryant recognized the desirability of the artist concealing himself behind his work. Here, after all, was the source of the "witchery" of art. The wonder and admiration of the reader are, these lines imply, best evoked by processes of which he is unaware. Like Hawthorne, who had compared the romancer to the weaver who works out the intricate patterns of his tapestry from the reverse side, Bryant saw that the secrets of the poet's craft were the more effectual for being somewhat mysterious. "The Poet," having hinted at these secrets and their source ("impassioned thought"), concludes with the highest tribute which the adoring public can bestow upon a poet:

> "What witchery hangs upon this poet's page!
> What art is his the written spells to find
> That sway from mood to mood the willing mind!"

II *The Expanding Sensibility*

To reconstruct the sensibility of a poet who consistently shielded himself behind the social masks of his day, who treasured the privacy of his gift, and who appeared at many times not to recognize his own genius is a task best undertaken through an examination of the poems themselves. Yet each poem seeks its context within a life-long development of the artist, a development which has its own laws and its own prerogatives. Such as it is, no series of generalizations can infallibly delineate the maturing processes of a sensibility; no pattern imposed upon it can explain its vagaries or its inconsistencies. At best, the phases through which it passes can be distinguished and the leading tendencies remarked.

Among all the theorists of sensibility, Emerson best understood its volatile nature and respected its organic quality. When, in the essay "Circles," he described the life of man as "a self-evolving circle, which, from a ring imperceptibly small, rushes on all sides outward to new and larger circles," he marked that special quality that the poet, above ordinary men, cultivates. Particularly is this true of the poet who writes in an open society that is relatively free from the taboos and rituals of tradition and who thinks, feels, and writes from his own immediate experience. The phases of his development shape themselves as concentric circles. For Bryant, as for many other American poets, the career in art was—as Emerson described it —"an apprenticeship to the truth that around every circle another can be drawn."[13]

What are the perceptible circles of Bryant's expanding sensibility? Five suggest themselves most clearly, and they should suffice for this study. The inner circle is that of the precocious young Bryant as he discovered the mysteries of language; the second, that of the young man (college student and barrister) who learns the quality of his peculiar vision; the third, the circle of intellectual awakening, in which ideas become immediate and distinct; the fourth, the phase which begins in his middle thirties in which he yearns for broader and more encompassing areas of experience, in which he travels, reads, and translates; the fifth, the outer circle, which may be named the circle of wisdom. Within this organic paradigm each of Bryant's poems falls into place and finds its proper relevance. Within it, we can relate, with some assurance, the inner man to his work.

The "imperceptibly small" circle at the center of Bryant's sensibility was that nurtured by the close family life at Cummington and Hampshire. Each of his parents left an indelible impression upon his sensibility, as did the years of schooling in the classics, the proximity of rich and abundant Nature, and the back-country religious orthodoxy. But his parents, especially, were foremost in his memory when he sat down many decades later to recount the days of his boyhood. His father was an intellectual and sophisticated man of the world who practiced medicine, read the classics, played the violin, and reveled in the political activity which took him often to Boston. His mother was devoutly religious, very close to her family and the land they had inhabited for several generations, attentive to her children, ambitious for them and for her husband. Most of all, both were parents who were talkers and writers—articulate persons who brought into the home the books and the visitors which would challenge the mind and the ear of any sensitive boy.

The poet, looking back on his childhood, attributed his early reading—the Bible at the age of four—to his mother's influence. He conjectures that "finding me rather docile, [Sarah Bryant] took pleasure in bringing me forward somewhat prematurely." He recalls also that she was, as was customary for pious New Englanders from the earliest days of settlement, a conscientious diarist who briefly noted each day the neighborhood gossip and her "simple occupations."[14] Through his mother's piety, most importantly, young Cullen was wrapped in the language of religious worship, its rhythms, its images, and its rhetorical structures. From his third year the boy attended church regularly, listened to the long sermons and the readings from Scripture, and sang the regular, rhymed hymns from the traditional Watt's *Hymnal*. And, lest the soul should lapse from grace, in the household of Squire Snell there were the evening and morning prayers, which Cullen, during his visits, attended.

The Calvinist theology passed by the boy, but the language did not. Remembering the particular beauty of some of these occasions of worship, Bryant described those who conducted the services as being "often poets in their extemporaneous prayers":

I have often, in my youth, heard from them prayers which were poems from beginning to end, mostly made up of sentences from the Old Testament writers. How often have I heard the supplication, "Let thy church arise and shine forth, fair as the moon, clear as the sun, beautiful as Tirzah, comely as Jerusalem, and terrible as an army with banners." One expression often in use was peculiarly impressive, and forcibly affected by childish imagination. "Let not our feet stumble on the dark mountains of eternal death." Then there was that prayer for revolution, handed down probably from the time of the Roundheads. "And wilt thou turn, and turn, and overturn, till he shall come whose right it is to reign, King of Nations, as of now King of Saints."[15]

For the poet who was to conceive and execute "Thanatopsis" these lofty phrases, the dignified but uncomplicated diction, and the rolling rhetoric were a profound influence. What had survived of the colonial "plain style" in which the Puritan clergymen had composed their sermons was to find its further extension in Bryant's blank verse, even though the promise of salvation concerned him little.

Through Dr. Peter Bryant, however, Cullen became familiar with language on a different level. No mere handmaid to Protestant piety, the language his father enjoyed was that of rational conversation, the play of wit, and the delightful and delicate harmonies which the classical poets had cultivated. The dull exercises of Latin and Greek in the schoolroom became the vehicles of beauty and wonder when his father recited passages from the ancients. The crabbed grammar and syntax thrust upon the student by his uncle, the Reverend Snell, became the weapons of the imagination and intellect when the good doctor directed his son to translate the third book of the *Aeneid*. At sixteen the boy responded to Virgil's forceful, melodic description of the tempest with a translation that reveals his well-developed sensitivity to verbs, to the interrupted line, and to the trisyllabic foot:

> While thus he mourns a roaring tempest strides,
> Fierce from the north, and rends its vessels sides,
> Tremendous surges, rising from the main,
> Aloft to heaven the labouring bark sustain,
> Its oars are shattered, and the waters ride,
> (Its prow inverted,) dashing on its side.[16]

But even earlier he had tested his métier and discovered the uses of wit in crude satires and lampoons. At twelve and thirteen he had written pastorals in the manner of the Augustan poets, including an "Ode to the Connecticut River." Absorbed in the magical play of assonance and alliteration, he gave voice to such experimental lines as these from "The Spring Walk":

> Again the vivid green I tread
> With garments fluttering in the gale;
> Or stretched beneath the deepening shade,
> The balmy breath of Spring inhale . . .[17]

Dr. Bryant had encouraged the boy in this direction, as well as toward the creation of the extended poem, "The Embargo"; but he also lent a sharply critical ear to the young poet's attempts at verse. On one occasion, Cullen, anticipating his father's praise, brought him an elegy beginning with the lines, "The word is given, the cruel arrow flies/With death-foreboding aim, and Woodbridge dies."[18] He was shocked, however, to learn "that it was nothing but tinsel and would not do." Thus, language—as it was subjected to the craft of the poet and exploited for its esthetic values—became, through this remarkable father, the poet's first and most valuable resource.

III   *The Circle of Vision*

Although his interest in, and aptitude for, language was to continue to grow, it ceased to dominate his poetry after his seventeenth year. By then he had entered fully his second circle and had begun to develop that faculty of vision that marks his mature verse. Vision is, of course, more than the sensory act of seeing; but it begins with the moment of conscious perception. Both his walks through the wooded countryside and his studies in botany had fastened upon him the habits of close observation, and it was from these visual experiences, impressed upon the mind sharply and in detail, that a number of his best poems were to be created. If the act of perception in itself had not carried its own authority, then Bryant's reading in the eighteenth-century philosophical psychologists Thomas Reid and Dugald Stewart,[19] who stressed the role of sensory perception in the acquisition of knowledge, would have brought the significance of his seeing before him. More and more, as he left behind him the bookish imagery and the fanciful scenery of the classical poets, he incorporated his own observation into his poems. Both his boyhood curiosity and psychological studies converged in the formation of a predominantly visual poetry. From 1818 to 1822 the bulk of his published poems, which were drawn from the visual experiences of his New England rambles, communicated the joy of discovering this second circle of sensibility. "The Yellow Violet" (1814, 1821), "To a Waterfowl" (1815, 1818), and "A Walk at Sunset" (1821, 1821) are all magnificent achievements of this type.

While the vision which Bryant cultivated during these years was partially the pure sensory experience—the recording of images upon the *tabula rasa* of the mind—it was also a creative act, engaging not merely the senses but the whole personality of the poet. The doctrine of the "association of ideas," as he had come across it in his reading, gave a plausible account of the way in which the mind, upon receiving sensory stimuli, associates them with experiences from the past. Wordsworth had responded to this psychology of association, and Bryant would seem to have read the *Lyrical Ballads* with growing interest from 1815 to 1820.

From Wordsworth, as well as from the theorists of the British school, the essential point was easily discovered: vision consisted not merely of the natural object directly perceived but also of the entire complex of feeling and thought which simultaneously arose in the poet. Thus, the phenomena observed on the long strolls took on fascinating new dimensions as the poet exercised his new-found capacity. By 1821 he had become adept in responding to Nature in this way. The vision of the sunset in "A Walk at Sunset" was not merely of the "thousand trembling lights" but also of the "bright isles beneath the setting sun"—the realms of death of which Indian lore had spoken. "The Rivulet" was not only a visible sign of Nature's carefree joy; it is also a reminder of the poet's lost youth—and the lost youth of the entire "fading race of men." Similarly, "The West Wind" becomes a symbol for the persistent melancholy of man, even in the midst of Nature's beauty.

Melancholy, in fact, is an almost inevitable product of the associationism in which Bryant engaged. The modern mind, alerted to the mysterious correlations between childhood and psychic disturbance, cannot help noting the constant recurrence of feelings of regret and guilt that are set loose by the process of memory. The guilt feelings occasionally emerge, as in "The Yellow Violet," but more often they are just beneath the surface, a shadow beneath the polished ice of the perfected verses. The themes of Bryant's poems tell us more than the passages in which explicit and rational thought is given its say; and these themes are predominantly those of death, loneliness, humility, and the passing of innocence. The association of ideas, set in motion by the act of seeing, is the process by which Bryant came to terms with the hidden core of his emotional life. The source of his anxieties remained obscure and repressed, but in such passages as the following (the italics are mine) we can observe how powerfully the simple act of seeing became for him a vehicle of intense and dark emotions:

> About this time [1809] occurred an event which I remember with regret. My grandfather Snell had always been substantially kind to me, and ready to forward any plan for my education, but when I did what in his judgment was wrong, he reprimanded me with a harshness which was not so well judged as it was probably deserved. I had committed some foolish blunder, and he was chiding me with even more than his usual severity; I turned and looked at him with a steady gaze. "What are you staring at?" he asked. "Did you never see me before?" "*Yes,*" I answered; "*I have seen you many times before.*" He never before had heard a disrespectful word from my lips. He turned and moved away. . .[20]

This steady gaze Godwin had found disconcerting upon first meeting Bryant, and the same expression is recorded in the portrait in oils by Samuel F. B. Morse. While the eyes look outward toward Grandfather Snell, journalists, and people at large, they also look inward, framing the immediate perception within the totality of the poet's experience. The words of impudence to his grandfather were half involuntary, expressing the kind of response to the moment which was better left to poetry. Henceforward the poet would, in social intercourse, remain mute behind this gaze, leaving to the sensible man of affairs which society had molded the business of maintaining human relations.

"To a Waterfowl" belongs to the outward circumference of the circle of vision.[21] In this poem, patently inspired by the personal observation of a wild bird at evening, perception evolves into an intricately structured response to experience. The eye, prompted by emotional conflicts of which the mind is only half conscious, turns inward, then outward once more—relating, mediating, resolving. The image of the bird becomes symbolic of the man who is also flying into the blinding darkness; who is, like the bird, dimly aware of the fowlers that stalk him; and who is also familiar with the immensity of the physical world. But deeper, at the core of the poem, and closer to the crux of the poet's disturbance, is the other symbol: that of the fowl's "solitary way" which is also the poet's "long way that I must tread alone."

The poem is really about the "way" of the lonely, isolated individual; and its entire structure forms itself about the poet's sense of motion through time and space. Each stanza of the poem deals intensely with one or another aspect of the "way"; each major shift in the development of the theme offers a new perspective upon the "way." Thus, the impact of the sensory impression upon the imagination of the artist is not fragmented and momentary but is distended through time until the mind sees not only the bird in flight but the continuous flight of the bird. In this poem all of the qualities of Bryant's vision are both fully realized and skillfully integrated.

To a Waterfowl

Whither, midst falling dew,
While glow the heavens with the last steps of day,
Far, through their rosy depths, dost thou pursue
Thy solitary way?

Vainly the fowler's eye
Might mark thy distant flight to do thee wrong,
As, darkly seen against the crimson sky,
    Thy figure floats along.

Seek'st thou the plashy brink
Of weedy lake, or marge of river wide,
Or where the rocking billows rise and sink
    On the chafed ocean-side?

There is a Power whose care
Teaches thy way along that pathless coast—
The desert and illimitable air—
    Lone wandering, but not lost.

All day thy wings have fanned,
At that far height, the cold, thin atmosphere,
Yet stoop not, weary, to the welcome land,
    Though the dark night is near.

And soon that toil shall end;
Soon shalt thou find a summer home, and rest,
And scream among thy fellows; reeds shall bend,
    Soon, o'er thy sheltered nest.

Thou'rt gone, the abyss of heaven
Hath swallowed up thy form; yet, on my heart
Deeply has sunk the lesson thou hast given,
    And shall not soon depart.

He who, from zone to zone,
Guides through the boundless sky thy certain flight,
In the long way that I must tread alone,
    Will lead my steps aright.

If "To a Waterfowl" is primarily a poem of vision, it also anticipates the next phase of Bryant's development as an artist. Only slightly submerged beneath the surface are the intellectual issues which many of his subsequent poems probe. There is, first, the questioning posture which always falls just short of agnosticism. There is, second, the belief in the God of Nature, the "Power whose care/Teaches thy way." Whether or not this Deity, responsible for the instinctive workings of animate Nature, is also a personal God, the patron of mankind, and the upholder of a moral order is a perennial problem in the poems of Nature. Third, there is the question of the internal division within man —the contention for supremacy between the reason and the heart.

These problems are resolved, of course, but only through the process of the poem itself. The fourth and eighth stanzas in "To a Waterfowl" are not pious platitudes; they are the efforts of the mind, and then of the heart, to relate within the context of the visual experience past certainties to present doubts, to formulate a purposefulness out of despair, and to control an environment which is obviously too complex and enormous for human manipulation. The *non sequitur* reply of the Reason in the fourth stanza, and the lessons imposed upon the heart in the seventh and eighth stanzas, are, let us admit, more courageous than honest, more noble than sane. But still there is an honesty, perhaps even a sanity, in this poem which is not the product of leisurely speculation on religious problems but which comes from the truth of a single experience—of a vision—which is the truth of the poet himself. Bryant's vision was unlike that of the seer or mystic who improvises epiphanies in unlikely places; his was the vision of discovery, the bringing to light of the secret, though sometimes obvious, truths of a man alive in the natural order.

The capacity to see continued to develop within the poet until Humanity as well as Nature could supply him with images. By 1825, in the *Lectures on Poetry*[22] he was to speak confidently of the "correspondences" and "analogies" of poetry and, by implication, to pay tribute to their centrality in his own work. He found in the landscapes of the Hudson River Valley painters, notably Thomas Cole, a visual and emotional equivalent of his own work. The etching by Asher B. Durand of Cole and Bryant standing together on a rocky platform, surrounded by underbrush and foliage, was significantly titled "Kindred Spirits."

IV *The Further Circles*

But beyond the circle of vision was the great circle of ideas. The poet had, of course, made tentative contact with the intellectual life early; and "The Embargo" demonstrates a speculative mentality. "Thanatopsis" is notable for its sage reasoning and for its neat argumentation. The real and the continuing enthusiasm for abstract thought, however, does not manifest itself until the poet has perfected his vision and has made contact with the heterogeneous cultures of Cambridge and New York City. The imagination of the poet, once secure in its operations, could assimilate the issues presented to it by the world.

The first of the great issues to engage the poet was that of death; the second, that of human progress. Each issue developed in its own way, at its own rate; and subsequent chapters of this study will deal with the place within the poet's work of these momentous themes. The poems of death, which fed upon the images supplied by the "graveyard poets," came to terms with the conflicting religious and scientific ideologies of the day, and in them the poet discovered a truly personal synthesis of vision and idea. The poems of progress drew heavily upon the political convictions of Bryant's liberal associates—Catherine and Theodore Sedgewick, John Bigelow, William Leggett—yet sought their meaning not in particular events, parties and programs, but in the broader perspective of the natural order of the universe.

In both the poems of death and the poems of progress there are, from work to work, the signs of resoluteness and of vacillation, of a great and compelling lucidity and of a sluggish banality, of a remarkable eagerness and of a melancholy resignation. There is no single attitude or idea which describes the body of poems dealing with either of these themes; there are only high points and low points, discoveries and evasions. For reasons that this study will explain in detail, the poems of death reached their apex quickly in "Thanatopsis" (1821), but the poems of progress postponed their full realization until their appearance in "The Fountain" (1839) and "The Antiquity of Freedom" (1842).

But both kinds of poems represent years of contemplation and experimentation. Each poem is a hypothesis to be confirmed in the crucible of the creative process. Each fresh insight has been measured by the ear, by the eye, and by the heart. In a sense these poems are synthetic, depending not upon their conceptual consistency alone but upon many elements of structure, metrics, and imagery. In a sense, also, there are no successes or failures among them, for each should be judged in terms of its contribution to the total expansion of the circle of ideas.

There are other ideas, of course, in Bryant's work. One can single out the themes of power, of innocence, of beauty, or of despair. All of these find their expression early in his career and reappear from time to time in varying configurations. As his vision took form, Bryant increased his capacity for reflection, and the crude statements of the intellectual novice are refined into the pure art of the major poems. Even the less sophisticated poems have their interest, for they often reveal the poet at work; he is attempting to break through his limitations and reach out toward fuller realization of his themes.

This outward thrust led him, over the years, to the broader circle of his maturity. About 1830 a new and different stability and firmness appear in his poems, and we find the ambitious young poet from the provinces responding to the richer, subtler culture of the city. The quality of mind is finer, less argumentative and more persuasive in such poems as "The Evening Wind" (1829), "To Cole, The Painter, Departing for Europe" (1829), "To the Fringed Gentian" (1832), and "The Prairies" (1832). His initial discovery of ideas had led him into overstatement; but—with time and experience behind him, with his place among the leaders of the American literary life secure, and with the stimulating prospect of new faces to see, new places to go, new ambitions to fulfill—his attitudes become less strained and his tone less extravagant. Over the years his maturity tended to become characterized by mellowness and relaxation, but the period beginning around 1830 and extending into the 1840's is one of vital and strenuous exploration.

To this period belongs his initial fascination with the wider horizon of European literature and the consequent urge for foreign travel. Translation had been habitual with him, and now, to his mastery of ancient languages, he added a knowledge of German, French, Spanish, Portuguese, Italian, and modern Greek. To the period 1830-43 belong the bulk of his translations from German and Spanish literature and his experiments with folk themes and ballads in imitation of European romantic poets. "The Song of Marion's Men" (1831), "Catterskill Falls" (1836), and "The White-Footed Deer" (1843) give evidence of his reading in European literature. "The Robber" (1835) and

"The Dark Lady" (1835) reveal his interest in the Gothic craze which had reached the American shores from England and Germany.

Try as he might, the boy from the Berkshires never became a true cosmopolite, but the expansion of his horizon kept him alive as a poet and established him—along with Irving, Cooper, and Longfellow—as a champion of a broader, more humane culture. Some of his aspirations toward the fuller life are projected in the poem "The Death of Schiller" (1838), which, in spite of the conventional sentiment of the closing stanzas, effectively focuses upon the *wanderlust,* that element of foreign Romanticism most attractive to the American writer—not only for Bryant but for Poe, Melville, and Hawthorne as well:

THE DEATH OF SCHILLER

'Tis said, when Schiller's death drew nigh,
  The wish possessed his mighty mind,
To wander forth wherever lie
  The homes and haunts of humankind.

Then strayed the poet, in his dreams,
  By Rome and Egypt's ancient graves;
Went up the New World's forest-streams,
  Stood in the Hindoo's temple-caves;

Walked with the Pawnee, fierce and stark,
  The sallow Tartar, midst his herds,
The peering Chinese, and the dark
  False Malay, uttering gentle words.

How could he rest? even then he trod
  The threshold of the world unknown;
Already, from the seat of God,
  A ray upon his garments shone;—

Shone and awoke the strong desire
  For love and knowledge reached not here,
Till, freed by death, his soul of fire
  Sprang to a fairer, ampler sphere.[23]

The accounts of his own inveterate traveling, which Bryant published in the *Post* and collected in the two volumes of *Letters of a Traveller*, hardly convey, however, the wish of a "mighty mind" to visit "The homes and haunts of human-kind." Bryant's writings in this field are inquisitive and critical, but their tone is journalistic and their content is more informative than inspirational. Reserved for the poems, notably "Earth" (1835) and "To the Apennines" (1835), was the kind of imaginative invasion of foreign ways that Bryant saw represented in Schiller's work. There are, however, too few of these poems; and it would seem that the strange power, that "witchery" of the poet, was too often suppressed in the American tourist. Bryant should have known that there was a difference between vision and sightseeing, but the recognition, if it did exist, was a dim and intermittent one. Travel appears to have been as much a result of the poetry of this middle period as a stimulant; and, while a few strong poems crystallize his response to foreign lands and incidentally uncover basic confusions and obscurities in his understanding of them, it is the aspiration and the longing for experience which give his work its momentum during this period rather than experience itself. Schiller's "wish" to wander, rather than the tourism of the journalist, is the key to the poetry of Bryant's "Middle Period."

Had Emerson developed to its ultimate conclusion his figure of concentric circles as they appear either in the pool or in vision, he would have noticed that the ultimate circle not only approaches the universality of Nature itself but also is a dissipation of strength and a blurring of vision. This is the paradox of Bryant's later poems: in their wisdom they lack the power that is generated by polarity and conflict. From the late 1840's, the pressure of the steady gaze diminishes. Although the command of verse technique persists and although the poet continues to bring image to idea and idea to image, the poems themselves are too easy to paraphrase, too quick to declare themselves, too sure of their tone and mood. By the time that Bryant was to compose "The Poet," he had long since passed the time when he wrote under the stimulus of deeply felt emotion. In "The Old Man's Counsel" (1840) he predicts the failure of his vision, and in "Among the Trees" (1868) he betrays his inability to respond to the living forces in nature.

Moments of conviction and new insights into the problems which had concerned him in his youth restored from time to time within his later years some of the former creativity; and, as a subsequent chapter will demonstrate, poems such as "The Death of Lincoln," "The Death of Slavery," and especially "October, 1866" have their own kind of effectiveness. There are also some remarkable lines and passages in poems that are otherwise weak. Bryant cannot be said, therefore, to have undergone the total decline which characterizes the careers of many American artists. The creative process, in becoming habitual, may have lost its sense of urgency; and, in spite of its willingness to adventure, it may have quickly reached its limitations—but the impulse was still there.

In reverting once more to the translation of foreign poets in his waning years, it was not to the works of the lyrical Romanticism that he turned, but back to the great classical poems of Homer. As even the least inspired of his later poems proved, his mastery over language never failed him. In the lines describing Ulysses' recovery from the storm in Book V, Bryant, recapturing some of the rhythm and imagery of "Thanatopsis," gave voice to a proper epigraph for his own creative life:

> So did Ulysses, in that pile of leaves,
> Bury himself, while Pallas o'er his eyes
> Poured sleep and closed his lids, that he might take,
> After his painful toils, the fitting rest.[24]

CHAPTER *2*

The Poems of Nature

IN ONE of the few passages in his poetry that explicitly personifies Nature, Bryant was to express his major insight into the meaning which the natural world had for him:

> To him who in the love of Nature holds
> Communion with her visible forms, she speaks
> A various language . . .

Though these lines are, of course, a prelude to a consideration of the theme of death, they could well serve as an introduction to Bryant's work as a whole. For the end product of his "communion" was not—as it was for many of his contemporaries —a pure delight, or solace, or simplification of life; but it was rather a "language"—a means of expressing those values and those moods for which no other means of expression was available. Just as he learned many foreign languages during his life, Bryant was to learn readily and sensitively the language of Nature. Like Wordsworth, he endeavored to look steadily at his subject; and, like Emerson, he sought for poetic material in the least of Nature's creatures as well as in the greatest. That duality of vision—by which his inward world became fused with the birds, flowers, trees, and mountains—Bryant developed early in his career and applied to the interpretation of the "visible forms" to which his lines refer. In his most successful creations, the act of communion became a dialogue in which Nature, although seldom personified, absorbed the poet's ideas and returned them to him, transformed and heightened.

This dialogue with Nature, it is true, had its deadly moments as well as its creative ones. In a poem like "Innocent Child and Snow White Flower" Bryant was capable of an easy, sentimental correlation between human values and natural objects which does justice to neither. For the most part, however, the correlations and analogies are not so facile; the poems gather intensity through the resistance of Nature to the glib moralizing of man. Though by temperament Bryant was not drawn to complicated and obscure matters, Nature had a way of thrusting upon him problems which were manifestly insolvable. The best poems grew out of no relaxed application of obvious sentiments to appropriate landscapes but out of a dynamic process in which the poet doubted as much as he accepted, resisted as much as he asserted, and denied as much as he bestowed. The "various language" which Nature spoke for Bryant was not always clear, nor was he consistently receptive; but it was the chief agency by which he was led into his poems—and into personal discoveries of meaning and value.

More specifically, there are four general areas into which Bryant's dialogue repeatedly ventured. (Two other major problems are treated in the following chapters on Death and Progress.) First, and most important for those who would distinguish between Bryant and the British Romantics, is his strong preference for the Nature to be found in the United States. Second, there is Bryant's consistent identification of beauty with the fragile transience of flowers. Third, there is the habitual association of romance with a natural or pastoral setting; indeed, there is an inability to conceive of it poetically in any other context. Fourth, there is his inclination to think of personal religion almost exclusively as a communion of man with God in Nature. Each of these generalizations is not a simple matter of attitude or opinion. In each of these areas the poet faced contradictions and paradoxes which are reflected in the poems themselves; and, only through an examination of specific poems, does Bryant's creative involvement with each of these issues become clear.

I American Landscapes

In considering, first, the preference of the poet for American native scenery, it is most useful to compare two poems in blank verse: one, a response to an American landscape; the other, a response to a foreign scene. The first, Bryant's widely anthologized poem "The Prairies" (1833), is perhaps his most enthusiastic paean to the New World. Only Whitman was to rival his vivid sense of American open spaces and to make it symbolic of the spread-eagle nationalism of the mid-nineteenth century. Yet even in this poem, Nature must have its say. The triumphant spirit which was, in 1833, already becoming that of Manifest Destiny would find its counter-spirit in the very imagery by which it was expressed. The experience of the moment—the artist's vision—served to correct the extravagances of political idealism. The poem is more than a piece of patriotic, breast-beating oratory; it recognizes values more inclusive and more profound than those of political slogans.

"The Prairies" was inspired, as Bryant's notes suggest, by his first exposure to the interminable stretches of land and sky to be found in the Great Plains. He had come upon them as he traveled westward to visit his brother, a settler in southern Illinois; and his reaction was immediate and intense.[1] The over-powering impression made upon him at this time is com-municated by the sweeping rhythms of the blank verse and by the sharp, plentiful imagery of the poem. Indeed, the pressures of spontaneous emotion upon the poet, as he set about composing this lyric, were great enough to make him forego his customary introduction and to dive into the substance of the poem with an emphatic "These . . ."

> These are the gardens of the Desert, these
> The unshorn fields, boundless and beautiful,
> For which the speech of England has no name—
> The Prairies. I behold them for the first,
> And my heart swells, while the dilated sight
> Takes in the encircling vastness.

From such paeans as this, of course, continental empires are made. The breezes that pass warmly across this plain

> have played
> Among the palms of Mexico and vines
> Of Texas, and have crisped the limpid brooks
> That from the fountains of Sonora glide
> Into the calm Pacific . . .

The nationalistic strain develops in lines of praise to distinctly American characteristics beyond those of topography: flora (high rank grass), fauna (Bison), and archeological evidences (those curious formations left by the mound builders). These mounds are, however, reminders of the insignificance of man's works in the universal scale; and the mood of the poet momentarily contends with the patriot's enthusiasm:

> Man hath no part in all this glorious work:
> The hand that built the firmament hath heaved
> And smoothed these verdant swells, and
> sown their slopes
> With herbage, planted them with island-groves,
> And hedged them round with forests.

Thereupon, these lines on the past gradually immerse the poet in less sanguine reflections on human progress:

> Thus change the forms of being. Thus arise
> Races of living things, glorious in strength,
> And perish, as the quickening breath of God
> Fills them, or is withdrawn.

Even this is not conclusive, however; and the flux of the poem—between the immediate majesty of the scene and the associations which it evokes in the mind of the historically conscious poet—continues. The overwhelming beauty, abundance and vitality of the scene before him draws the poet out of the past into the immediate experience of the present:

> Still this great solitude is quick with life.
> Myriads of insects, gaudy as the flowers
> They flutter over, gentle quadrupeds,
> And birds, that scarce have learned
> the fear of man,
> Are here, and sliding reptiles of the ground,
> Startlingly beautiful.

Such delight, continues this dialogue of the poet with Nature, can only promise a rich future. The pervasive sound of the bees, a "domestic hum," is converted by the imagination into the other noises of eventual settlement:

> The sound of that advancing multitude
> Which soon shall fill these deserts.
>   From the ground
> Comes up the laugh of children, the soft voice
> Of maidens, and the sweet and solemn hymn
> Of Sabbath worshippers.

Again the historical consciousness wanes, the vision of prosperous nationalism fades into the perception of the moment, and Nature speaks once more her "various language": "All at once/A fresher wind sweeps by, and breaks my dream,/And I am in the wilderness alone."[2]

With this radical reversal in mood, the poem closes, leaving the reader suspended between the alternative ideas and emotions which the poet has extracted from his experience. "The Prairies" is, thus, illustrative of Bryant's treatment of Nature in his better poems, particularly those in blank verse; but it differs from them in one important respect. It is one of the few poems which takes place in the open solitude rather than in the intimate glade or brook-side retreat. Nor is the perspective of the poem that of the fashionable "picturesque" with those neat, rectangularly framed vistas that the eighteenth century had enjoyed. Rather the vision, which Bryant describes as that of "dilated sight," is a vision of plenitude as it pours in upon the sensibility from all sides, a fullness of experience in the face of which the poet can only record the ebb and flow of his emotional life.

All in all, "The Prairies" is a very convincing and compelling work, not because it is the springing to life of a hypothesis—the greatness and promise of America—in an appropriately spontaneous fashion, but because it is a complete realization by the poetic intelligence of what it means to entertain this hypothesis. Bryant was not, as Whitman was to be, temperamentally or intellectually ready to take the optimistic plunge into the benevolent cosmos. His dream must break, leaving him "in the wilderness alone." But this is the source of the poem's strength, even though it may be a source of philosophical confusion. If the sublime esthetics of the national spirit were one order of truth which the poet could express through the medium of natural imagery, there was another order of truth which placed man, as an autonomous consciousness, apart and isolated from the natural phenomena which he perceived. "The Prairies" does not reconcile these truths, but it forcefully expresses the dilemma of the romantic sensibility as it sought political conviction in a dream of America, the Beautiful.

"Earth," composed two years later in 1834, approached the problem of national sentiment in an entirely different manner. The sensibility of the poet encountered not a vast stage for heroic enterprise in Nature but a formless and ominous night. The historical consciousness, instead of providing a release from the immediate scene, tended to intensify a melancholy experience. The imagery, instead of conveying a vivid sense of natural detail, was blurred and dusky. As the first strophe suggests, "Earth" is closer to Matthew Arnold's "Dover Beach" than it is to Whitman's "Passage to India":

> A midnight black with clouds is in the sky;
> I seem to feel, upon my limbs, the weight
> Of its vast brooding shadow. All in vain
> Turns the tired eye in search of form; no star
> Pierces the pitchy veil; no ruddy blaze,
> From dwellings lighted by the cheerful hearth,
> Tinges the flowering summits of the grass.
> No sound of life is heard, no village hum.
> Nor measured tramp of footstep in the path,
> Nor rush of wind, while, on the breast of Earth,
> I lie and listen to her mighty voice:
> A voice of many tones—sent up from streams
> That wander through the gloom, from woods unseen
> Swayed by the sweeping of the tides of air,
> From rocky chasms where darkness dwells all day,
> And hollows of the great invisible hills,
> And sands that edge the ocean, stretching far
> Into the night—a melancholy sound!

Why the eye is "tired" and why the "mighty voice" of Earth is melancholy seem to be explained by the memory of past wars, injustices, bloodshed, and terror. Even the "glens and groves" now "murmur of guilty force and treachery." The poet's consciousness of the past merges with his memories of personal grief. He attempts to identify his sorrow with that of Earth and thus find expression for his own depression in Nature's language:

"O Earth! dost thou too sorrow for the past/Like man thy offspring? Do I hear thee mourn/Thy childhood's unreturning hours . . . ?"

Yet this process of identification is too costly, for it plunges the poet from one level of despair deeper into murky areas from which he is hard put to recover. At one point the language verges upon the erotic, as the images of Earth and the dead loved ones are momentarily synthesized: "Alone, in darkness, on thy naked soil,/The mighty nourisher and burial-place/Of man, I feel that I embrace their dust."

In the lines immediately following, however, this implicit longing for death is replaced by a deeper murmur at which the poet begins to "tremble at its dreadful import." Nature throws back upon him not merely the evil of the historical past but also what seem to be references to personal guilt: "The dust of her who loved and was betrayed,/And him who died neglected in his age . . ."[3] Line after line the images of wronged humanity accumulate to provide a Gothic gallery for which there would seem to be no atonement, no resolution, no compensating mood.

Yet the ready answer had been spelled out in "The Prairies" and in numbers of other poems. Nature in the Old World was soiled by civilization; Nature in the New World gave promise of bright things to come. The concluding strophes of "Earth" seek an equilibrium for the poem in this comforting idea. Thus, the key to the poem, delayed until this crucial moment, is now provided:

> Here, where I rest, the vales of Italy
> Are round me, populous from early time,
> And field of the tremendous warfare waged
> 'Twixt good and evil. Who, alas! shall dare
> Interpret to man's ear the mingled voice
> That comes from her old dungeons . . .

Earth has not, after all, spoken—only the "mingled voice" of those historical excrescences to be found in "the vales of Italy." Yet even if this murmur with which the poet has conducted his dialogue is not that of Nature in its pristine purity, the issue has been raised: Is there hope that mankind can ever outrun its history and return to the state of moral innocence—even in the brave New World?

Bryant attempts, not altogether successfully, to answer this question with a qualified "yes." The mood of the poem as a whole is not easily ignored, and his affirmation is reduced to a rather pallid rhetorical question:

> O thou,
> Who sittest far beyond the Atlantic deep,
> Among the sources of thy glorious streams,
> My native Land of Groves! a newer page
> In the great record of the world is thine;
> Shall it be fairer? Fear, and friendly Hope,
> And Envy, watch the issue, while the lines,
> By which thou shalt be judged, are written down.[4]

Together, "The Prairies" and "Earth" illustrate the potential strengths and weaknesses of Bryant's efforts to test his patriotic assumptions in a creative experiment. Although these poems are quite different in many ways, they both encounter a language of discovery; and, in consequence, each acquires a complexity and distinctiveness quite unusual in patriotic hymns.

II *The Transient Flowers*

Simple emotions were not Bryant's forte. The almost prosaic language of his verses and the general clarity of the dramatic situations of the poems are too often deceptive. Even his little verses on flowers, unpretentious and subdued as they appear, are not pure expressions of delight and admiration. Inhibiting the emotional impulse which brings the poet to the exquisite and delicate subject matter of violets, gentians, and windflowers is not only the artist's sense of form but also an intelligence alert to physical and moral relationships. Instead of simplicity, these poems contain an involvement and intricacy which is their real merit. And furthermore, what they may lose in lyrical power is often compensated for by the poet's insight into the fullness of his experience.

That these poems can be read—and too often are—as polite sketches with appended moral sentiments is unfortunate; and yet such misinterpretations reflect Bryant's own dilemma in the face of natural beauty. Does Nature, after all, unite beauty and moral truth within the same discernible objects, or are there two quite distinct orders of value? At times Bryant writes as though beauty necessarily entails some sort of certitude and has its own authority; but the more successful poems, three of which shall be briefly treated here, imply that it is the imagination of the poet and the human capacity to formulate experiences into art which ultimately unifies value with perception, truth with beauty.

Best known of these three is "The Yellow Violet," composed when Bryant was twenty years of age. Central to this quiet lyric is the idea that this blossom appears in April as a harbinger of spring. The opening stanza accurately pin-points the time of year and briefly captures the visual image of the flower as it is found in its natural habitat:

> When beechen buds begin to swell,
>   And woods the blue-bird's warble know,
> The yellow violet's modest bell
>   Peeps from the last year's leaves below.

The second stanza introduces the speaker in the poem and imposes upon the scene his rather vague emotion: "Sweet flower, I love, in forest bare,/To meet thee. . . ." From this point through the remaining six stanzas, the poem is—as Professor George Arms has suggested—essentially dramatic.[5] The flower and narrator are participants in a dialogue which rises to a disclosure and eventual climax. Neither the intrinsic beauty of the flower nor the poet's delight upon discovering it lie at the heart of the verses, but instead the subject is an awareness, which is all but mutual, of the degree of human pride involved in any observation of natural forms:

> Oft, in the sunless April day,
>   Thy early smile has stayed my walk;
> But midst the gorgeous blooms of May,
>   I passed thee on thy humble stalk.
>
> So they, who climb to wealth, forget
>   The friends in darker fortunes tried.
> I copied them—but I regret
>   That I should ape the ways of pride.[6]

Simply to pass this off as "moralism" is to miss the unfolding of the poem and its play of delight against reflection. Does the violet remind the poet of guilt incurred in his social relations, or does the metaphor of the social climber serve to explain man's neglect of the humble beauties of nature? To reread these lines with this question in mind is to grasp the complexity of Bryant's esthetic. My answer is that the poem has it both ways and that this is the essence of the dramatic dialogue. Thus, the concluding stanza can be read, both literally and figuratively, as a statement about man's moral relationship to Nature *and* as a comment upon one's social obligations:

> And when again the genial hour
>   Awakes the painted tribes of light,
> I'll not o'erlook the modest flower
>   That made the woods of April bright.

Complementary to "The Yellow Violet," to the extent that it deals with the last lingering blossom of autumn instead of the first to appear in spring, is "To the Fringed Gentian." There are no feelings of regret aroused by this flower; in fact, four of the five stanzas sing clearly and sweetly of its blue brightness and of the cold, bare setting in which it appears. Although the plant is apostrophized, there is no intrusion of the first person pronoun and no imposition of the speaker's feelings upon the subject matter—until the final stanza. There the rational element, staved off for sixteen lines, must have its say. Moved by the barrenness of the passing year to consider his own demise and "the hour of death," the poet sees in the flower an emblem of "Hope, blossoming within my heart." The full text of "To the Fringed Gentian" is as follows:

> Thou blossom bright with autumn dew
> And colored with the heaven's own blue,
> That openest when the quiet light
> Succeeds the keen and frosty night—
>
> Thou comest not when violets lean
> O'er wandering brooks and springs unseen,
> Or columbines, in purple dressed,
> Nod o'er the ground-bird's hidden nest.
>
> Thou waitest late and com'st alone,
> When woods are bare and birds are flown,
> And frosts and shortening days portend
> The aged year is near his end.

Then doth thy sweet and quiet eye
Look through its fringes to the sky,
Blue—blue—as if that sky let fall
A flower from its cerulean wall.

I would that thus, when I shall see
The hour of death draw near to me,
Hope, blossoming within my heart,
May look to heaven as I depart.[7]

The metaphor which equates Hope with the blue flower crystallizes an entire train of reflection which has run submerged through the poem. The concern of the narrator for the desolation of approaching winter, his feeling for the solitary nature of the flower, and his association of the flower's blue with that of the heavens have all been steps toward the realization expressed in the final lines. The statement of moral meaning may be overly explicit, but it is by no means gratuitous: it comes as the fruit of the observation and reflection of a human being strongly infected with the quality of a late autumn walk. Not only do these lines extract human meaning from a chance contact with the fringed gentian, but also do they cast back upon Nature itself a solemn appreciation of its dignified movement through the cycle of life and death. For the poet, in his restrained appeal that he, too, might die as Nature dies (with hope for regeneration), has added a further dimension to the experience. The small flower and its local setting are perceived within some greater context—call it Time—in which both men and natural objects move. This appeal of the poet is, thus, a delayed recognition of the empathetic relationship between man and flower.

In the third of these flower poems, "The Death of the Flowers," Bryant has used a similar structural device. Instead of delaying his articulation of the theme of the poem, however, he withholds the key to the dramatic situation. By skillful treatment of the autumnal passing of the summer flowers, he creates a fine balance between pathos and detachment. The eventual, inevitable passage of beautiful things is established as the theme of the poem; and the full sense of what is meant by the opening line, "The melancholy days have come, the saddest of the year," is developed in every line. The third stanza, for example, sustains the mood while offering only the slightest hint ("the plague on men") as to the basic situation:

The wind-flower and the violet, they perished long ago,
And the brier rose and the orchis died amid the summer glow,
But on the hill the golden-rod, and the aster in the wood,
And the yellow sunflower by the brook in autumn beauty stood,
Till fell the frost from the clear cold heaven, as falls the plague
   on men,
And the brightness of their smile was gone, from upland, glade,
   and glen.[8]

Thus, the disclosure in the fifth stanza that the proper object of the lament is not the flowers—that they have only served as symbolic substitutes for the young girl who has died—does not come as a shocking surprise but as an honest recognition of the inexorable bond between beauty and death. The imagery of the flowers, the mood of early winter, and the rhythms set in motion by the descriptive verses give to this concluding stanza of "The Death of the Flowers" a restrained tension which is a marvelous achievement. The effect is that of the slow rising to conscious articulation of buried, inexpressible grief and of the vast sense of relief which comes from the poet's ability to objectify the experience:

And then I think of one who in her youthful beauty died,
The fair meek blossom that grew up and faded by my side.
In the cold moist earth we laid her, when the forests cast the leaf,
And we wept that one so lovely should have a life so brief:
Yet not unmeet it was that one, like that young friend of ours,
So gentle and so beautiful, should perish with the flowers.

III *Romance in Nature*

The use of natural imagery in this poem as a means for describing the feeling attendant upon the death of a beautiful young girl introduces one of the most muddled and baffling aspects of Romantic poetry. The beautiful girl, so runs one line of thought, is Nature's innocent child—Wordsworth's Lucy —whose loveliness derives from qualities quite apart from her sexuality. Yet she dies. Is it the awareness of the gross complexity of the world that kills her? A disdain for her animal nature?

Or is it the divine rule of Nature (as we find it expressed in "The Death of the Flowers") that beauty passes in a day and is gone? The entire subject is shrouded in conflicting ideas and emotions, but the poet finds in this very ambiguity the kind of material his imagination requires. Here is a more profoundly ethical poetry than that of "the land" or that of floral beauty. Using his proper tools of imagery, structure, and rhythm, the poet sifts the values and feelings relating to romance in the modern world. Out of his own divided feelings about natural man (*Is there a natural woman also?*), about chastity (*Is it of God and Nature?*), and about the involvement of love with passion (*Can the higher be reached without the lower?*), Bryant fashioned his lyrics of young maidens in Nature.

Representative of one extreme position, and widely anthologized, is "Oh Fairest of the Rural Maids," a rather polite and unambitious piece of flattery directed toward Miss Frances Fairchild, who subsequently became Bryant's wife. In the convention of Renaissance love lyrics, the adored name is immortalized in the poem, albeit somewhat coyly divided and spaced (italicized) in the first and fifth lines:

> Oh *fair*est of the rural maids!
> Thy birth was in the forest shades;
> Green boughs, and glimpses of the sky,
> Were all that met thine infant eye.
>
> Thy sports, thy wanderings, when a *child*,
> Were ever in the sylvan wild;
> And all the beauty of the place
> Is in thy heart and on thy face.[9]

The association of the "sylvan wild" with feminine beauty passes unquestioned in this poem. No instance of Nature more violent than the playful wind or the quiet spring arises to shatter the pretty comparison. But perhaps there is a lingering doubt—at least the concluding stanza takes pains to relate the untraveled forest to the young woman's innocence:

> The forest depths, by foot unpressed,
> Are not more sinless than thy breast;
> The holy peace, that fills the air
> Of those calm solitudes, is there.

Thus, the compatibility of natural beauty and moral purity are upheld through bland assertion. There is, however, a trace of equivocation in the awkward expression "Are not more sinless," and a straining for the image in "foot unpressed," by which the undefiled quality of the female breast is described.

Other poems partially retract this absurd commitment to the absolute sinlessness of the female sex. The children of nature in "An Indian Story," "Monument Mountain," and "The Strange Lady"—all Indian maidens—are plagued by terror and guilt as no flaxen-haired, blue-eyed rural maids could ever be. In portraying the stirrings of passion within these female characters, Bryant seems to have drawn, especially in "The Strange Lady," upon the romantic stereotype described by Mario Praz as *La Belle Dame Sans Merci*. For the most part, however, these Indian characters, although subject to the pains of passion, are devoid of malignance and cruelty.

The poem in which Bryant's matured treatment of Nature and sexuality occurs is "Monument Mountain," a fine work in several ways. Although there are imitative elements in it, the poem is remarkably vivid in its setting, consistent in its synthesis of human and natural elements, and of an almost classical deliberateness in its movement toward the fatal close. The tale, which gives the poem its structure, is simply that of an Indian maiden, "bright-eyed/with a wealth of maiden tresses."

> She loved her cousin; such a love was deemed,
> By the morality of those stern tribes,
> Incestuous, and she struggled hard and long
> Against her love, and reasoned with her heart,
> As simple Indian maiden might.[10]

After prolonged suffering she confides her troubles to a friend, saying: " 'Thou know'st, and thou alone,'/ . . . 'for I have told thee, all my love,/And guilt, and sorrow.' " Her confession made, she puts on the ornaments her father had given her, climbs with her friend to the precipice on the mountain which commands "the region of her tribe," and, at sunset, throws herself from the rock.

It is a tale with Hawthorne's darkness about it; and, like Melville's novel, *Pierre*, which it may well have inspired, "Monu-

ment Mountain" treats the subject of incest in such a way that
innocence itself is made the source of grief and guilt. Also,
like the major works of Hawthorne and Melville, this poem is
unified by a dominant central symbol: the mountain which
derives its name from the monument of rough stones placed there
by the mourning tribes. The mountain symbolizes Nature, not
only, as we might expect, in its permanence and immensity, but
also in those qualities of beauty and savagery as they are
paradoxically combined in natural objects: "Thou who wouldst
see the lovely and the wild/Mingled in harmony on Nature's
face,/Ascend our rocky mountains."

And what is true of Nature, is also by implication true of
natural man. Though the climber of the mountain may achieve
an "expanding heart," "a kindred with a loftier world," and
"The enlargement of . . . vision," the experience is not one
of tranquility but an imposing mixture of peace and terror,
loveliness and wildness. Even while the eye takes in "white
villages, and tilth and herd," it also sees "bare old cliffs," seared
by the elements to "chalky whiteness":

> . . . It is a fearful thing
> To stand upon the beetling verge, and see
> Where storm and lightning, from that huge gray wall,
> Have tumbled down vast blocks, and at the base
> Dashed them in fragments, and to lay thine ear
> Over the dizzy depth, and hear the sound
> Of winds, that struggle with the woods below,
> Come up like ocean murmurs.

The sensibility, nourished by these contradictory aspects of
the scene before it, turns to the tale—the "sad tradition of un-
happy love" to find a relevance to human experience.

The poem develops dramatically from this point, tracing the
impact of the outlawed desires of the maiden upon her body
and her spirit. She who once was "The fairest of the Indian maids,
bright-eyed,/With wealth of raven tresses, a light form,/And a
gay heart," loses her gaiety, weeps in solitude, and wastes away
until the sage dames of the tribe say, *The girl will die.*" To her
closest friend she pours out her heart:

> . . . I am sick of life.
> All night I weep in darkness, and the morn
> Glares on me, as upon a thing accursed,
> That has no business on the earth.

The natural passion of the innocent has, as she herself recognizes, become unnatural. Only through death can she return to a state of harmony with Nature. Only death restores the balance between her beauty and her wildness.

Her suicide has its own solemn ritual: the ascent of the mountain, the wearing of ornaments associated with childhood and happier days, the day-long vigil on the mountaintop overlooking "the region of her tribe," and, particularly "the cabin-roof/Of him she loved." Indeed, this is a religious rite, for the location of her vigil, the precipice, is strewn with offerings to the tribal gods. The Indians believed "that God/Doth walk on high places," and so they share, in a more direct and primitive fashion, the feelings of exaltation of the civilized climber with his "expanded heart" and enlarged vision.

Much later in his career, Bryant reworked the theme of lost innocence into a fantasy, "Sella" (1862). This tale in blank verse tells of a young maiden, Sella, who discovers a pair of magic slippers in which she may descend beneath the surface of the stream near her family home. There, throughout her young years, she explores the wonders and beauties of submarine life; and, under the guidance of a nameless, exotic fairy, she travels downstream into the great ocean. Her parents, when they hear from her of these excursions, decide that she is a dreamer; but her brother, motivated by fear and envy of "that cold world of waters and the strange/Beings that dwell within it," eventually steals the slippers and throws them into the stream—forever out of reach. Sella accuses her family harshly, in a tone which suggests the Indian maiden's lament:

> . . . Cruel ones!
> 'Tis you who shut me out eternally
> From that serener world which I had learned
> To love so well. Why took ye not my life?[11]

However, this thinly veiled story of sexual awakening, also hinting of an incestuous relationship, comes to a happier conclusion than "Monument Mountain." Sella finds a less catastrophic penance in acts of mercy, and she gains new strength through prayer. Her innocent adventures bear strange fruit, for she becomes a philosopher-queen, instructing her people in the mysteries of hydromechanics and teaching them to build venetian wells, viaducts, and water wheels. Throughout her life, however, she remains celibate; and, upon her death, she is buried near the stream of her childhood, under a marble monument inscribed with her name. The stream subsequently divides to flow over the grave.

The contrast between "Monument Mountain" and "Sella" does not reflect any substantial shift in Bryant's treatment of sexuality. In both poems the metaphor of ascent (the Indian maiden climbs the mountain, while Sella emerges from the fantasy world of the sea) indicates the capacity of human beings to transcend their limitations, either self-imposed, as in Sella's case, or instilled in the conscience through tribal mores. In both poems the emphasis is upon the moral and emotional conflicts within the individual rather than upon any romantic or sexual contact between the girl and her lover. Indeed, the implication of these two poems is that sexuality is almost entirely an intimate, personal problem in which the loved one or society at large has little stake. Chastity is not glorified as a social ideal but as a personal standard gleaned from some contact by the uncorrupted innocent with the spiritual laws governing the universe. What distinguishes the two poems and explains the different endings is a change in Bryant's attitude toward guilt and retribution. Whereas the Indian maiden could expiate her sinful passion only through the ultimate gesture expressive of her faith, Sella was to be cleansed through a doctrine of works. But theological conceptions were foreign to Bryant; and, aside from the apparent influence of the Civil War upon his life and art, it is difficult to assess this shift in his attitude.

IV *Piety in Nature*

In a sense, all of Bryant's poems of Nature are traceable to a concern for religious values. That this should emerge more explicitly in these two poems, where the dominant theme is the role of sexual emotion in nature and society, than it had in the poems dealing with national vistas or flowers, suggests that the deeper the poet mined his heart, the closer he came to the religious ore. The religious problem, however, even as it crops up in Nature poetry, is not an isolated one. Though its balance and texture are derived from the personal experiences of the poet, these experiences take place within the larger context of his immediate society. Thus, his personal religious feelings and ideas—particularly as they are expressed in "A Forest Hymn," "Inscription for the Entrance to a Wood," and "A Summer Ramble,"—bear the imprint of the intellectual revolution which had taken place in late eighteenth- and early nineteenth-century New England.

As the historians have made abundantly clear, the breakdown of the monolithic intellectual system of Calvinism in New England and the passing flurry of enlightened Deism in the late eighteenth century had left large vacuums in the religious lives of the Protestant middle class with which Bryant identified himself. In particular, there was lacking the vital center of emotional conviction, without which neither the remnant disciples of the old Puritanism nor the liberals, chief among whom were the Unitarians, could hope to survive. Although the function of revivalism in prolonging the life of the Calvinist genus is not our proper concern here, it was one means by which emotionalism, "enthusiasm" in the theological terminology of the day, could be respectably reinstated into community life. It provided a convenient bridge, as Wordsworthian lyricism was also to do, between the narrow sphere of private piety and the communal ground of institutionalized society.

The liberal churches did not, quite naturally, turn from Bible and sacraments to the pursuit of the God of Nature, and thus too rigorous a parallelism between pietistic revivalism and lyric poetry can only obscure our point. What was held in common was a motive rather than a practice: a sense that American individualism meant more than an atomistic relationship between members of the body politic—it meant that the individual could become emotionally and intellectually, for certain heightened moments at least, the receptacle of the living universe. The great metaphors of revivalism—Jesus the Redeemer, Salvation, Heaven—penetrated to the core of personal life as the doctrines of the Atonement, Predestination, and Election had, by 1800, ceased to do for the mass of men. On the other hand,

the liberal consciousness, its initial awe of a Newtonian machine-
universe rubbed thin, turned to an image of the Creator with
which the heart might make contact, a beneficent Father whose
construction of the natural order, according to the revealed laws
of physics, was accompanied by generous good-will toward men.
William Ellery Channing set the tone for nineteenth-century
Unitarianism, but such hymns as "The Earth is full of Thy
Riches," written by Bryant while still at Great Barrington in
1820, lent further support to the movement to unite science with
sentiment:

> ALMIGHTY! hear thy children raise
> The voice of thankfulness and praise,
> To Him whose wisdom deigned to plan
> This fair and bright abode for man.
>
> For when this orb of sea and land
> Was moulded in thy forming hand,
> Thy calm, benignant smile impressed
> A beam of heaven upon its breast.[12]

Even though our analysis is too general to do justice to the
complex social history of the early nineteenth century, it does
shed considerable light upon the lyricism of Bryant's poetry.
For, like the revivalist, Bryant had no new theology—not even
a novel *Weltanschauung*—to offer, only new life to breathe into
accepted conceptions. As Whitehead and others have observed,
Romantic poetry about Nature may have resisted the mechanism
of eighteenth-century science, but the magnificent vision of a
universe made orderly and whole remained undiminished. Thus,
Bryant differs from an enlightened poet like Freneau not because
he rejects natural philosophy, but because his lyricism travels
further down the road of personal involvement with the facts
of nature. True, he stopped short of the kind of organic relationship with natural facts of which Emerson was to preach and
of which Whitman was to sing; and he thus remains the natural
philosopher rather than the Transcendentalist. His involvement,
however, prompts him to break through the scientific abstractions which define the order of nature in a way that Freneau,
even in "The Wild Honeysuckle," could only approximate. And
in this convergence of poetry with natural fact, which also

entailed the dissipation of "scientific" systems, classifications, and simple cause-and-effect relationships, a genuine and deeply felt reverence for things was born. In the face of nature on his rambles and in the brookside meditations, the rational knowledge of the poet first gave way to sensation, groped its way back toward understanding, and then unified the stream of experience within his poem.

The failure of our contemporary readers to respond to Bryant's pious Nature poetry is symptomatic. Science, having long since abandoned the obvious evidences of order—such as would strike the eye of Sunday strollers or bird watchers—has left us indifferent before natural objects, save for those which overwhelm us with sensory stimuli. For the nineteenth century, however, still laboriously sifting genera and species, still pondering the enormous scale of geological ages, still deciphering the mysterious laws which govern comets, natural facts were neither too remote to be interesting nor too complex to forestall rational consideration. Thus it was that the magnificent "Creator" or "First Cause" of Newton could be glimpsed, in moments of intensity, only a few paces beyond normal vision, lurking behind woodland oaks and impelling birds in their flight. It does no real harm if modern critics and scholars thrust the label of pantheism upon this poetry; one form of heresy is, I suppose, as good as another. What must be borne in mind, nevertheless, is that Bryant's *theology* differs in no essential way from the Christian rationalism of the eighteenth century. Not systematic thought brought him closer to God, and God closer to Nature, but mood, revery, and observation. This piety which we cannot share had its source not in logic but in experience, and only thus can it be comprehended.

From this critical perspective, poems such as "A Forest Hymn," "Inscription for the Entrance to a Wood," and "A Summer Ramble" become confessions rather than credos. They are, after all, neither statements of faith nor philosophical treatises; they are accounts of an individual as he faces Nature in search of religious illumination. The philosophical framework is just that—a framework—for within it mood, reflection, and speculation play in a highly unpredictable fashion.

The synthesizing process by which Bryant created these poems is most evident in "A Forest Hymn." Fundamentally a reasoned statement in verse about the appropriateness of worshiping God in natural surroundings, this poem gathers a particular drive of its own as it develops; and it soon discards argumentation as its structural device.

The rational abstractions serve their purpose, however, in providing a firm, credible foundation for the highly personal superstructure. Protestants would find familiar contrasts between the ways of simpler virtue and "human pomp or pride." They would find intellectual satisfaction in the argument that the woods are a purer place of worship than man-made edifices because "No fantastic carvings show/The boast of our vain race to change the form/Of thy fair works."[13] The mind could agree that the values of "grandeur, strength, and grace" are exemplified in the natural objects to be found within the forest. In the life-and-death cycle evidenced by the mold of decaying vegetation there is, certainly, "The lesson of thy own eternity." Though there have been "holy men" who have given themselves up to lives of "thought and prayer" in the wilderness, it suffices, says the voice of moderation, to retire "often to these solitudes." And, finally, the forest serves as a distinct reminder of the tokens of God's power—tempests, whirlwinds, and tidal waves—all of which tame man's pride and return him to a realization of God's omnipotence.

As a series of abstractions these statements are vaguely satisfying, voicing as they do the convictions of a liberalized Protestantism. But it is in the diction of this poem, rather than in its structured argument that feeling brims with precision and intensity. Particularly in the second division of the poem, immediately following the lines on "the boast of our vain race," the poet breaks from his moralistic moorings to address a God directly perceived; the poem moves from a hymn to the First Cause to a lyric prayer to the personal deity of the poet:

> . . . But thou art here—thou fill'st
> The solitude. Thou art in the soft winds
> That run along the summit of these trees
> In music; thou art in the cooler breath
> That from the inmost darkness of the place
> Comes, scarcely felt; the barky trunks, the ground,
> The fresh moist ground, are all instinct with thee.

It is with the "barky trees" that observation sharpens; and, in the phrases reflecting the process of contemplation itself—"the ground,/The fresh moist ground"—the accumulation of natural fact begins. In rapid succession follow a bird, herbs, the spring, an oak, each absorbed into the generalization regarding God's presence, but also recreating the experience of private communion with Nature. The last lines of this division press to its ultimate bound the poet's apprehension of the spiritual reality of the occurrence within the forest scene:

> That delicate forest flower,
> With scented breath and look so like a smile,
> Seems, as it issues from the shapeless mould,
> An emanation of the indwelling Life,
> A visible token of the upholding Love,
> That are the soul of this great universe.

This is the core of piety in a poem which might otherwise have been merely conventionally religious. This is the momentary baring of the vital center of the religious life. That the doctrine of immanence runs counter to the poet's rational convictions regarding the order of the universe and the status of natural objects as "tokens" of the Creator's power and goodness signifies the imaginative vitality of the poem. Within the context of "The Forest Hymn" this momentary perception makes perfectly good sense; for of what use is the return to Nature's temple if God is not there? Emerson and Whitman, once the way had been made clear, could raise to the level of reflective affirmation the idea that "love works at the centre" ("The Sphinx") and "the kelson of the creation is Love" ("Song of Myself"). For Bryant, the discovery was the fruit of the imaginative process, not its premise; and it had to be won anew with each successive lyric.

When read with this principle of discovery in mind, "Inscription for the Entrance to a Wood" and "A Summer Ramble" lose some of the staleness which nineteenth-century poetry has for many readers. "Inscription" begins with a plea for the "Stranger," tired of the "guilt and misery" of the world, to "enter this wild wood/And view the haunts of Nature." It briefly develops the proposition that "God hath yoked to guilt/Her pale tormentor, misery," and it draws the questionable conclusion (invalid, if restated as a syllogism) that, being without guilt, "these shades/

Are still the abodes of gladness." With this expression, however, the liberal theology fades and sensory delights pour in upon poet and reader until reflection is almost totally in abeyance, leaving the quality of the experience itself to reign unchallenged.[14]

Similarly in "A Summer Ramble," once the formal recognition is made that "the plants and breathing things [are] The sinless, peaceful works of God," there is no longer reference to the Deity by name, realist overwhelms nominalist, and "the lovely landscape round" speaks for itself. It is the "deep quiet" of the tranquil scene, as the final lines declare so simply, that this "Shall be the peace whose holy smile/Welcomes him to a happier shore."[15]

Even while this lyric piety before the things of God's Nature liberated the poet from human suffering and conflict and from the confines of the ratiocinative process, it also made for limitations and restrictions. The paradoxes implicit in the representations of patriotic scenery, of beauty in nature, and of natural woman should also have indicated the fruitful perversity of the language of Nature. But there is no more blatant, or embarrassing, example of the inner contradictions created by Bryant's attempt to fuse natural religion and human values than in his poem titled "Hymn of the City."

To judge this poem by the standard of the author's intent is to deem it a failure. "Hymn of the City" is obviously intended to complement "A Forest Hymn" and to make the point that:

> Not in the solitude
> Alone may man commune with Heaven, or see,
>   Only in savage wood
> And sunny vale, the present Deity . . .
>
> Even here do I behold
> Thy steps, Almighty!—here, amid the crowd
>   Through the great city rolled . . .[16]

But how is God made evident in the city? Only by comparison between the details of city life and the familiar imagery of Nature can the voice of the Deity be heard. The sound of the "winds whisper and the waves rejoice" finds a substitute in the noise of the crowd—the "everlasting murmur deep and loud." While the physical substance of the city is passed off as "proud piles, the work of human kind," the concluding stanzas of the poem are rich with the imagery of sun, sea, and tempest. And to confirm our suspicion that it is not really the bustle of the crowd which reveals God's spirit, the coda of the poem describes the city in its eventual return to harmonious solitude, "vast and helpless" while it sleeps.

In a later, more honest appraisal of the city, "The Crowded Street," Bryant weighed the balance heavily against urban life and emphasized the pervasive sense of futility and indifference of the city dwellers. For neither the orderly values of scientific rationalism nor the esthetic pieties of Nature worship were applicable to the new industrial civilization. Not until Whitman's "Crossing Brooklyn Ferry" was a poem to appear which could successfully incorporate urban images and rhythms in a meaningful synthesis.

If Nature poetry was to draw much of its power from religious experience, however, it faced the great dilemma well known to the saints and mystics of the West. Subsequent to the tidal flow of illumination must come the slow ebbing of grace. What has been lived can only be remembered, not relived; the poet, like the saint, must seek his inspiration in time as best he can. Bryant revealed, in passages, a partial recognition of such a waning sensitivity. Both "The Old Man's Counsel" and "Among the Trees" have rather fine lines recognizing the pathos of this loss. In the former, the old man compares the perceptual life to the rising crescendo and gradual diminution of the love-signal of the partridge. Life in its later stages, like a boat on the rapids, "Darts by so swiftly that their images/Dwell not upon the mind, or only dwell/In dim confusion. . . ."[17]

"Among the Trees" (1868), on the other hand, is the attempt of the aging poet to recapture his lost sensibility. It opens in the familiar setting of trees and springs, and it apostrophizes the trees in the conventional manner; but, instead of building toward a moment of lyric realization, the poet conducts an unanswered monologue:

> Have ye no sense of being? Does the air,
> The pure air, which I breathe with gladness, pass
> In gushes o'er your delicate lungs, your leaves,
> All unenjoyed? When on your winter's sleep
> The sun shines warm, have ye no dreams of spring?[18]

And so on for another twenty-one lines—the plight of articulate man in the face of his dumb environment. Lacking his answer, the poet resorts to half-hearted affirmation, but the lyric compulsion has passed him by:

> Nay, doubt we not that under the rough rind,
> In the green veins of these fair growths of earth,
> There dwells a nature that receives delight
> From all the gentle processes of life,
> And shrinks from loss of being. Dim and faint
> May be the sense of pleasure and of pain,
> As in our dreams; but, haply, real still.

The remainder of the poem develops, with some success, two leading ideas: first, the lack of sympathy that Nature holds for man ("Our sorrows touch you not."); and second, the superior survival power of natural objects ("Ye have no history."). These melancholy themes, even though lacking in complete integration into this poem, look forward to the material of twentieth-century poetry.

Difficult as it is to find convincing passages of true lyricism in his later poetry, the God of Nature which Bryant had worshiped in his youth did not disappear with the years. Thus it is that, drawing from the writings of Boethius, he could write in the 1860's (in the decade following the publication of *The Origin of Species*) these triumphant lines from "The Order of Nature."

> While the Great Founder, he who gave these laws,
> Holds the firm reins and sits amid his skies
> Monarch and Master, Origin and Cause,
> And Arbiter supremely just and wise.
>
> He guides the force he gave; his hand restrains
> And curbs it to the circle it must trace:
> Else the fair fabric which his power sustains
> Would fall to fragments in the void of space.[19]

Theology intact, in spite of his loss of personal contact with Nature, he could still speak boldly and militantly of the harmony and order of natural law.

The thesis of this discussion—that Bryant found in Nature

a "various language" through which he was enabled to conduct a dialogue and embark on a series of "discoveries"—has implications which extend far beyond Bryant or his poems. That it says something about Romanticism, both in the United States and in Europe, that it relates to the search for a style on the part of the modern artist, that it probes at the hidden roots of Transcendentalism—both as an esthetic theory and as a religious philosophy—will be evident to the students of literature and of the history of culture. Later chapters shall be more directly concerned with several of these implications; but, for the present, it will suffice to recognize the poems of Nature for what they are: the products of an active, creative imagination as it explored the possibilities of expression to be found in the hypothesis that Nature was language. Even a partial recognition of this element in the poems will make obsolete the notion that Bryant wrote a kind of descriptive verse to which he affixed sentiments palatable to his readers. The case is a strong one that Bryant composed the bulk of his work as a synthesis of his deepest feeling and most serious thought. It is in this spirit which his poems deserve to be considered.

CHAPTER 3

The Poem of Death

THE OPENING LINES of "Thanatopsis" explicitly announce
that the poet's dialogue with Nature is central in this great
poem. Yet the theme of death—death as it pertains immediately
and personally to the poet—introduces elements which set this
relationship between man and Nature apart from those examined
in the previous chapter. This theme, by virtue of its concern
with the problem of consciousness, calls into question not only
the meaning of the dialogue but the very possibility of its being
conducted at all. For the dialogue was founded upon the
assumption that all experience contains two absolute ingredients:
a subject and an object. Bryant was never to criticize this
inviolate dualism instilled in the Western mind by Descartes and
Locke, and even those moments of ecstatic insight to be found in
the religious poems were to respect the sharp distinction between
the observer and the observed, between the poet and Nature,
between consciousness and material fact. But death, which
destroys consciousness, ignores this distinction. Its presence—or
even the threat of its presence—seems to deny the existence
of a separate, autonomous sensibility capable of standing apart
from its environment. The grave with its dank, dissolving
remnants of humanity is the symbolic answer of that implacable
monist—Nature—to all of the poet's inquiries and speculations
concerning death.

Thus, to the difficulties already inherent in Bryant's creative
process, the theme of death added philosophical and artistic
problems of a much wider scope than he encountered in his
other poems. Only in "Thanatopsis" was he able to rise above
the involvements and contradictions posed by this theme. Only
in "Thanatopsis" was he able to adapt the dialogue and the

loose associationism of his blank verse to a structured, consistent discourse. The other poems about death, as the subsequent discussion shall point out, were fragmentary, equivocal, or, at best, evasive in their handling of this theme. Why "Thanatopsis" survived its trials while the others failed is not easy to determine, but the key to its mastery and power seems to lie in its curious career of premature publication and consistent revision. As this chapter will explain, Bryant's progress through at least three versions of the poem during half a decade lured him deeper and deeper into its heart. The ultimate product, "Thanatopsis" as it emerged in the 1821 edition of his poems, was a curiously synthetic work composed of a number of quite unstable elements held in a state of artistic equilibrium.[1]

I Contrasts with Christian Attitudes

The crux of the poem is, as many commentators have recognized, that there are consolations for the inevitable end of human existence quite aside from the Christian promise of eternal life. The greater part of "Thanatopsis" is a summary catalogue of these consolations, both human and natural, which are sufficient to sustain and soothe the individual as he approaches the grave. "Thanatopsis" is not a refutation of the doctrine of immortality. Although it is obviously addressed to the sensibility of those who have found scant comfort in this doctrine, the poem completely avoids any confrontation of religious problems, either on the theological or on emotional levels. The problem successfully attacked in "Thanatopsis" is not what happens to the soul in death but to the human mind.

And it is a mistake to read into the poem either our personal religious doubts or to attribute to Bryant, in this instance, any heretical denial of basic Christian doctrine.[2] The tendency of criticism has been to equate the shifts in Bryant's attitude toward death, culminating in "Thanatopsis," with his espousal of liberal religion. But the fact is that his hymns written for the Unitarian hymnal assert at several points the doctrine of immortal life, and they thus establish beyond question Bryant's personal belief. The hymns share with "Thanatopsis," as we shall see presently, the deliberate omission of moralistic attitudes toward death, but otherwise are completely different in their orientation. The hymns are suppliant addresses to God; "Thanatopsis" is a dialogue with Nature.

For Bryant to divest himself completely of the Christian concepts, even for artistic purposes, was no easy matter; for his childhood religious background, his reading in the so-called "graveyard poets," and his respect for established modes of thought, all conspired to lead him directly from experience into ontological problems. Indeed, the irony of the poem is that so much from the Christian tradition is freely borrowed to express an exclusively secular point of view. Yet out of his materials Bryant fashioned one of the few major works that speaks directly to the rationalist, empiricist mentality. "Thanatopsis" is a complex poem not because of any obscurity or ambiguity—Bryant was nothing if not lucid—but because it places a pungent, new wine in old and mellow bottles. Its comprehensive statement about death, still satisfactory today to many intellectuals, was somehow fashioned out of bits and pieces of biblical lore, pulpit oratory, and pious verse. The artistic success was hard-won, for both thought and sentiment tended, it seems, to follow well-worn ruts. Yet the poem's limited point of view and its carefully restricted emotional appeal remained inviolate as each successive revision defined the problem more closely and, ultimately, brought to it a satisfying resolution.

Bryant's use of his materials is further illustrated by his literary borrowing from two poems which he was reading at approximately the same time he began "Thanatopsis." Both of these are staunchly orthodox in their theology. Bishop Porteus' "Death" praised, in Augustan imagery and meter, a Christ who had taught men how to die by his noble example. Robert Blair's "The Grave" evoked a long parade of ghostly horrors before dramatizing the conquest of Death by the Redeemer. Bryant had, incidentally, preferred Blair to Porteus; he cited the "superior originality in thought and vigor of expression" of "the finer passages" in "The Grave."[3]

The presumptive evidence is strong that one of these "finer passages" from Blair was the following: "What is this world?/ What but a specious burial-field unwalled,/Strewed with Death's spoils. . . ."[4] Bryant in "Thanatopsis," referring to the earth as "one mighty sepulchre," was to describe the hills, sea, and other scenic natural objects as "the solemn decorations all/Of the great tomb of man." If Blair's tone had been one of gothic horror, Bryant's was one of meditative calm. Similarly, in "Death" there are the lines in which Bishop Porteus, lapsing into the heavy irony of the pulpit moralist, had written: "In Fancy's fairy paths/ Let the gay songster rove, and gently trill/The strain of empty joy."[5] In "Thanatopsis" the poetic idea becomes:

> . . . The gay will laugh
> When thou art gone, the solemn brood of care
> Plod on, and each one as before will chase
> His favorite phantom; yet all these shall leave
> Their mirth and their employments . . .

Thus, Bryant would derive from verses, which not only were tediously didactic but also drew upon clear theological assumptions, the ingredients for his highly original message. On the one hand, a metaphor expressing the contempt of orthodox Protestantism for things of this world is converted to laud the abundant beauty of Nature; on the other, the disdain for frivolous amusement expressed by Bishop Porteus is muted by placing both gaiety and industry on the same plane.

But there was another element of Christian thought which made stronger claims upon Bryant's imagination. Several of his earlier poems had focused upon the retributive aspects both of death and of life beyond the grave; and, while Bryant had no vision of a heaven or hell, the idea that divine will manifested itself through the taking of life had an undeniable fascination for him. In 1815 he had written the poem known as "Not That From Life and All Its Woes," in which the following lines appear:

> There is a sacred dread of death
> Inwoven with the strings of life.
> This bitter cup at first was given
> When angry *justice* frown'd severe,
> And 'tis th' eternal doom of heaven
> That man must view the grave with fear.[6]

Bryant's "Hymn to Death" (1820) subjects this idea to its crucial test. Death is glorified throughout the early portions of the blank verse as a "Deliverer" appointed by God "to free the oppressed/And crush the oppressor." Although men have slandered Death, naming him the "king of terrors," an "assassin," or "the spoiler of the world," the poet asserts that "I am come to speak/Thy praises." But the poet's excesses were cruelly corrected before he had completed the poem: Dr. Peter Bryant had died:

> Alas! I little thought that the stern power,
> Whose fearful praise I sang, would try me thus
> Before the strain was ended. It must cease—
> For he is in his grave who taught my youth
> The art of verse . . .
>
> . . . Shuddering I look
> On what is written, yet I blot not out
> The desultory numbers; let them stand,
> The record of an idle revery.[7]

This poem reveals Bryant at his experimental best, seeking for the tone and argument that he could finally accept among a variety of alternatives.

From its inception, "Thanatopsis" moved in a radically different direction from that which visualized Death as an agent of divine retribution. But even in "Thanatopsis," in a fugitive passage that was soon stricken from the manuscript, the complementary doctrine of divine mercy was alluded to: "By the kind hope that mercy will accept/Perfect the imperfect duties of thy life/And pardon all thy errors. . . ."[8] Only the tightest discipline kept his perspective and subject directly before the poet. The moral assumptions of Christianity were, in large part, his assumptions also.

II Contrasts with Sentimental Attitudes

However, there were poetic visions of death other than those based upon orthodox Christianity. As Carl Van Doren pointed out nearly fifty years ago, "Thanatopsis" was an answer to the frantic questioning of the poetry of Henry Kirke White, a British poet of the late eighteenth century. Bryant's response to Kirke White's morbid lyrics was, as remembered in his reminiscences, enthusiastic: "I read the [*The Remains of Kirke White*] with great eagerness, and so often that I had committed several of them to memory, particularly the ode to Rosemary. The melancholy tone which prevails in them deepened the interest with which I read them, for about that time I had, as young poets are apt to have, a liking for poetry of a querulous cast."[9]

Mr. Van Doren rightly commented that the young Bryant had taken the deeply wounded question of Kirke White, "Who will hear of Henry?" more closely to heart than he had the pat affirmations of religion.[10] He imitated this poet's neurotic apprehensiveness in such lines as "The cold clods press thy limbs above,/The darkness and the worm are there."[11] And he located with even greater precision than Kirke White did the source of their common anxiety in an over-conscious subjectivity:

> They taught me, and it was a fearful creed
> That God forgets his creatures in the grave
> And to the eternity of darkness leaves
> Thought and its organs. Fearful upon my heart
> Fastened the terrible doubt—and the strong fear
> Of death o'ermastered me . . .
>
> And all that I had learnt of virtue here
> In the world's suffering—all that studious toil
> Had taught me—all that from the book
> Of Nature I had striven to transcribe
> Into my mind—and from the laid-up thoughts
> Of men of other days had now no place—
> Parted—blotted out forever. . . .[12]

Even allowing for some youthful posturing, these lines cast considerable light on the final version of "Thanatopsis," and they explain the urgency of the fears—for which Nature would have a rebuttal—in the introductory passage:

> . . . When thoughts
> Of the last bitter hour came like a blight
> Over thy spirit, and sad images
> Of the stern agony, and shroud, and pall,
> And breathless darkness, and the narrow house,
> Make thee to shudder, and grow sick at heart. . . .

Not the concern for eternal life, nor the prospect of damnation motivated these lines. The problem was one for natural man alone to face and to resolve without the palliatives of religion. How was the autonomous mind to accept its annihilation?

If Bryant drew part of "Thanatopsis" from a poetry of questioning despair, he drew another part from a poetry of facile assertion. The conception of Nature as a maternal figure, implicit throughout the early lines of the poem, and the language of the final lines are echoes of a verse by Mrs. Lydia Sigourney—the Sweet Singer of Hartford. This work, "A Versification of a remark by Pliny," appeared in the same issue as the early version of "Thanatopsis" (prior to the addition of the pertinent lines), and it is characteristic of a shallow sensibility at work on the same theme. According to Mrs. Sigourney, Earth is distinctive among the various forces in Nature. Unlike the hostile elements, Earth sustains man like a mother and provides him "with a couch of rest at his death." In spite of the buffets of life, natural man is not totally forsaken, and the great Mother has her maudlin eye upon him:

> Yes, earth, kind earth, her new-born son beholds
> Spreads a soft shelter, in her robe enfolds,
> Still like a mother kind, her love retains,
> Cheers by her sweetness, with her food sustains,
> Paints her fair flowers to wake his infant smile,
> Spreads out her fruits to sooth his hour of toil. . . .

And, in a final piece of grotesque imagery, the Earth accepts man as a corpse: "She to her arms, her mould'ring son receives,/ Sings a low requiem, to her darling birth,/'Return! thou loved one, to thy parent earth'."[13]

Bryant rejected the sentimental assumptions of Mrs. Sigourney, of course, but he borrowed her images and phrases. The appearance of "sustained and soothed," for example, in "Thanatopsis" connotes no fanciful activity of an improbable Earth but rather the moral and psychological state of one who is about to die. While Mrs. Sigourney's poem relies upon an easy acceptance of a benevolent Nature, Bryant comes to terms with a number of hard facts about human life. Whether or not he was entirely successful in this instance of literary borrowing is, however, an open question. For some critics, these maternal and tranquilizing connotations are never fully integrated into the hard, stoic message of the poem as a whole. Does Nature speak with two voices, one philosophical and one sentimental? The issue is central to any critical assessment of "Thanatopsis," as our subsequent discussion of the poem's meaning and structure will indicate.

III Career of "Thanatopsis" Through Its Revisions

But first the curious sequence of events which brought about this synthetic poem should be considered. Upon certain of these events, present knowledge is incomplete; but the broad outline is reasonably clear. At the age of twenty-one and at the time when Bryant was completing his study of the law, the topic of death powerfully stimulated his imagination. He not only had been reading Kirke White and the other poets of a "querulous cast," but he also had experienced a local epidemic, a suicide in his neighborhood, the death of the bride of one of his close friends, and the severe illness which had struck both the poet and his father during the winter of 1814-15. All of these had induced speculative thought on the brevity of human life. During this period Bryant composed several poems about death, including not only "Not That from Life, and All Its Woes," but also "A Chorus of Shades," the latter of which contains a number of images similar to those of "Thanatopsis." Furthermore, the influence of his reading in Wordsworth had begun to manifest itself by 1814 in the pastoral subject matter of his poems and in the relaxation of the iambic stress in his blank verse. It seems reasonably certain that, as Professor William Cullen Bryant II has argued in an excellent article, the first version of "Thanatopsis" in blank verse was composed *circa* 1815.[14]

The next stage in the poem's development was its publication in the September, 1817, issue of the *North American Review,* a relatively new periodical edited by those whom Dr. Peter Bryant considered the "literati" of Boston. Dr. Bryant had been urging his son, then a busy, young lawyer, to submit his poetry to the *Review,* but by the summer of 1817 Cullen had shown no inclination to do so. Taking matters in his own hands, the doctor copied several poems which his son had left in a desk and took them to Willard Phillips, a friend of longstanding and one of the editors of the journal. Charles Henry Dana, another member of the original board, is supposed to have read these poems with such amazed admiration that he momentarily doubted that they could have been composed by anyone on this side of the Atlantic.[15] Two poems were immediately published in the September issue—"Thanatopsis" and "Not That From Life and All Its Woes"—and two others appeared subsequently—"Inscription for the Entrance to a Wood" and "To a Waterfowl."

In addition to its being rushed into print before its author had completed it to his satisfaction, "Thanatopsis" suffered two further accidents in the process of publication. The first has already been commented upon: the proximity in the issue of Mrs. Sigourney's verse on a similar subject. The second, which has puzzled generations of critics, was the printing of the four rhymed quatrains known as "Not That From Life, and All Its Woes" as an introduction to the blank verse. Perhaps Dr. Bryant had copied both poems on a single page, or perhaps the editors, noting that both poems were literally "about death," saw nothing wrong in combining the regular and blank verses. In either case, Cullen Bryant must have been struck by the obvious conflict between the attitudes toward death conveyed by these quite different poems, and yet he may also have noticed the appropriateness of providing the blank verse with some sort of introduction. These are merely conjectures, but it is significant that the poet, shortly afterwards, took up the problem of revising "Thanatopsis" along these two same lines. The subsequent revisions progressed toward a firm refutation of the theme of "Not That From Life and All Its Woes" expressed in the lines: "And 'tis th' eternal doom of heaven/That man must view the grave with fear." And each revision attempted to introduce "Thanatopsis" in such a way that the consolations for death emanated from a single identified source.

Bryant's central problem as he revised his poem was this matter of the source of his consolations. And yet the structure of his poetic method clearly limited the alternative sources of his "voice"; there were only two parties to the poet's dialogue with Nature. Either the speaker had to be man himself—obviously the most interested party—or it had to be Nature, who was, perhaps too disinterested. On the other hand, what was there about the relationship between man and Nature which qualified either participant in the dialogue to speak on this crucial matter, much less to offer compelling consolations? The dilemma was unavoidable. At last the young poet had struck upon material which resisted his talent and challenged his philosophical outlook. The two subsequent revisions, the second of which became the final text, groped toward both truth and form.

In the nine lines which begin the revision of 1818-20 (designated as Manuscript B by McDowell[16]), the consolation emanates from the "better genius" of the poet. Nature acts merely as a catalyst, reminding man of his mortality. But the dialogue itself is internal and introspective, as the higher faculties of the poet spout philosophy to the mortal flesh.

These nine lines had been—possibly—part of the earlier manuscript and thus their appearance in Manuscript B may be no more than the young poet's refusal to acknowledge the editorial tampering (by his father?) which had prevented their appearance in the *Review*. But whether the lines were, *circa* 1818, being salvaged from an earlier version, or whether, in the poet's conception of his work, they had never been deleted, they were still a meaningful option to him up to those months of 1821 that he spent in Cambridge preparing his poetry for the first volume of collected works.

The possibility that these lines which follow were rejected as inferior verse cannot be overlooked, particularly if Dr. Bryant had found them wanting. Their diction, imagery and rhythms are, however, quite consistent with "Thanatopsis" as a whole; and it seems unlikely that Bryant would have discarded such potentially rich material in its entirety unless their controlling idea was inadequate. These introductory lines run:

> It was his better genius that was wont
> To steal upon the bard what time his steps
> Sought the repose of nature, lone and still
> And unfrequented walks—and in his ear
> To whisper things of which it irks the mind
> That clings to the dead fallacies of life
> To think:—and gravely with his graver hours
> Oft the benevolent and heedful one
> Would thus commune ——

What was it that made the voice of the "better genius" unacceptable to Bryant? Several alternatives suggest themselves. First was the undisguised subjectivity and implied intuitionalism of this approach, which stressed those elements of imported Romanticism least attractive to the American reader. Even twenty years later, Emerson's appeal to the "genius" latent within all men was to fall upon hostile, if not deaf, ears. Throughout Bryant's poetry, the interior life is corrected by the exterior life, or, at the very least, the racial life anterior to the individual. Although Bryant would share with Emerson an antipathy to certain kinds of authority and although he reserved the right to question the "truths" imposed upon him by reality, he was never to grasp the full implications of the doctrine of self-reliance. Indeed, his very use of the idea of "better genius" in these lines is less Transcendental than Byronic, more introspective than intuitive.

Yet even the introspective tone had its weakness, quite apart from the philosophical implications. For, as Bryant might well have recognized, this is the tone of self-pity and of egotistic anxiety. Nature's solitude and beauty relieved men of their low view of life and introduced an element of the sublime into even the most prosaic activities and thoughts. Thus it was inappropriate, and perhaps actually insensitive, for the poet to seek the repose and stillness of Nature, only so that he might better hear his own voice, as, indeed this earlier version of the poem has it. And a further but less significant objection to the "better genius" is that it left Bryant without any meaningful conclusion to his poem. Given his lack of full confidence in the inner voice, the problem of resolving its dilemmas in any suitable artistic fashion was nearly impossible. Though he tried to make the consolations stick—in one draft by reasserting the universality of death; in the other by a last minute assertion of Christian sentiments—there was lacking the firmness and formal strength which consolations, if they are to succeed at all, must have.

IV *The Voice of Nature*

If such difficulties lay in this direction, why did not Bryant immediately seize upon the other alternative? Why did he delay for five years before making the consolations spring from the voice of Nature? The answer to these questions is suggested by the contrast between "Thanatopsis" and the poetic effort of Mrs. Sigourney. The danger that Nature might be reduced to human proportions through such personifications as that of Mrs. Sigourney was even greater than the danger of subjectivism.

Nature was, by Bryant's unspoken definition, the great movement of time through all the transient phenomena of the material world. That Nature, so defined, should concern itself with the passing of consciousness was not immediately plausible, for what is consciousness but the perception of the phenomenal flux? Nature as environment, no matter how sublimely conceived, would have no consolations for the minor discomforts which its great work may have occasioned. Only the sentimentalist could detect in the murmur of this magnificent machine any acknowledgement of man's significance in the scheme of things.

We cannot know that Bryant considered the problem of revision in exactly these terms, but his alterations show him as first choosing Nature as his voice, and then going a step further than was his usual practice in establishing the philosophical base upon which his poem was to be founded. Nature was more than environment; Nature becomes, in Baudelaire's famous phrase, *un forêts de symboles.* The dialogue of the poet was not merely with his environment but with the "visible forms" through which a higher wisdom is communicated. In "Thanatopsis," as in no other poem, Bryant was driven to recognize that his poetic dialogue was no simple dialectic between subject-Man and object-Nature; it was instead an involved process of creation in which physical objects and poetic images were not easily distinguishable. That Nature might herself project a metaphorical language, no better than the vision which changes its focus from one poem to the next, was the unique realization of "Thanatopsis": "To him who in the love of Nature holds/ Communion with her visible forms, she speaks/A various language. . . ."

Throughout the poem this emphasis upon the differences between "forms" and some sort of transcendent reality reoccurs. The "pale form" of line 20 and the "fair forms" of line 36 both refer to the material remains—the corpse of the poet. The sufferings of a dying man are, as conceived by the poet, "sad images." In line 64 human beings are described in terms which connote the illusory quality of life: ". . . and each one as before will chase/His favorite phantom. . . ." And the concluding statement of the poem, which occurs only in the final draft, defines decisively the limited role of visual perceptions, whether they be "forms," "images," "phantoms," or, as in this case, "pleasant dreams": ". . . approach thy grave,/Like one who wraps the drapery of his couch/About him, and lies down to pleasant dreams."

In contrast to the aberrations of sight, however, are the verities of sound. Not the sounds of sense perception, it is true, but the mysterious words which the Old Testament prophets had heard emerging out of the burning bushes and whirlwinds of their symbolic surroundings. Like Grey before him and Tennyson after,[17] Bryant seized upon the provocative paradox of the "still voice," and in the context of "Thanatopsis" made it a credible source of his consolations for death. For the poet as listener, in contrast to the poet as seeker or visionary, was all that the poem needed. The dialogue was maintained, albeit somewhat one-sidedly; and the vastness of Nature was not diminished through a trivial metaphor. Bryant could have his visual imagery, yet deny it, too, as the very lines in which the still voice occurs demonstrate:

> Go forth, under the open sky, and list
> To Nature's teachings, while from all around—
> Earth and her waters, and the depths of air—
> Comes a still voice—

The power and meaning of "Thanatopsis" hang by this slender thread. Rational consciousness and natural piety are both satisfied by this simple, allusive device. The dialogue, seemingly threatened by the absorption of consciousness into the perpetual cycle of Nature, has been restored on a deeper level of understanding than that implied by the other poems of Nature. For the assumption upon which all of the consolations of the poem are based is that the faculty of human reason—while it may operate independently of Nature and achieve a degree of self-realization—can never enter into a dialogue with Nature on equal terms. That Nature speaks to man through forms—including his own "pale form"—and with a "various language" indicates the limitations of human understanding. Indeed, it is this insight, with its suggestion of Hebraic prophecy, which motivates the entire development of the theme of "Thanatopsis." The human reason is gently persuaded to abandon its presumptuous claims to uniqueness and autonomy. Death is to be recognized as a fulfillment of the life of partial knowledge—not as the termination of an absolute consciousness. The dialogue no longer assumes that the voice of man is capable of bouncing echoes off an objective mountain; it proceeds in the understanding that the very images, words, sounds, and ideas projected by man are merely chips and slivers from a monumental wholeness and truth. Although the dialogue is still functional in the poem, the poet at last has been awed into a tentative silence while the "still voice" of universal wisdom has its say.

V Sermon as Structure

However, this reversal—or inversion—of the customary direction of the dialogue posed formal problems even while it solved intellectual ones. The blank verse could no longer drift on the currents of the poet's revery. The poet could no longer apostrophize and interrogate, as he had in "To a Waterfowl." Nor could he turn inward upon his personal experience, as he had, for example, in "The Yellow Violet." To the contrary, the formal requirements were, first, a clear progression of ideas toward a definitive conclusion; second, a calm, authoritative voice which spoke not merely to the poet in his privacy but to all receptive men; and third, a language which would apply universal truth to the commonplace.

Each of these requirements had been met by a rhetorical style which Bryant, throughout his youth, had encountered Sabbath after Sabbath. The old "plain style," imported to New England by the earliest settlers, had been preserved in the small towns of white clapboard houses through nearly two centuries of theological strife. And the sermon in the plain style was as eminently lucid as the village steeple in its architectural development, unmistakably structured according to a tripartite division into *doctrine, reason,* and *uses.*[18] Its voice was that of the chosen man of God who applied his gifts to further explanation of God's word as revealed in scripture. Its language was simple and homely. In the words of Thomas Hooker it would "make a hard point easy and familiar in explication."[19] Although Bryant may not have been aware that the plain-style sermon was the form he sought, its applicability was clear enough. Consciously or not, "Thanatopsis" became a Romantic sermon.

The division of the poem into three parts is clearly indicated by the stanzaic patterns. The first section (through line 30) establishes, in lieu of revealed truth, the authority of Nature as it speaks through the "still voice" and as it offers the "doctrine" that man is to lose "each human trace." The second section (lines 31-72), in a close analogy to the *reasons* by which the Puritan divine would convince his listeners of the rational basis of the *doctrine,* argues persuasively against the objections which men raise to their deaths. The third section (lines 73-81) applies the theme of the poem—just as the *uses* of the plain style sermon had applied the message of the scripture—to the ordinary course of human life. Like the seventeenth-century divine, Bryant prefaced his rational consideration of the human plight with an appeal to a higher authority, and he concluded it with a direct application to the moral life. This simple, sturdy form—which had brought a vigorous clarity into the religious life of American Protestantism—instilled into "Thanatopsis" its own rugged genius. The indigenous culture of Bryant's native land had contributed, in a fashion unsuspected by either his admirers or his detractors, to the formation of a poetic master-piece, the first created since the founding of the Republic.

As our knowledge of the various stages through which "Thanatopsis" passed clearly shows, the realization of this tripartite form was the final, decisive phase. Only in Cambridge, two and one half years after the poem had appeared in the *North American Review,* did the voice of Nature emerge to state its doctrine, or did the poet recognize that his personal reflections on death had led him to the inescapable moral conclusion of the final lines. The poem expanded almost of its own accord into a readily available form. Although the sermon form was by its own nature rigid and inelastic, its adoption was the result of an organic process of composition. The revision of "Thanatopsis" was no mere matter of patching and padding; it was an evolution of thought and feeling toward an ultimate goal. Perhaps the goal was implicit in the language of Manuscript A in the passage evoking the burial of the human body and the loss of sensate functions. Perhaps the argument "Yet not to thine eternal resting place . . ." which we have compared to the *reasons* of the plain style sermon, demanded a more disciplined framework than that provided by revery and undirected blank verse. In any case, the successive manuscripts reveal Bryant moving through various alternatives toward a final version of his poem—a version in which thought and form are gracefully united.

VI *Contrasts in Intent and Tone*

A recognition of the broad outlines of the Puritan sermon in "Thanatopsis" does more, however, than reveal a subliminal means for achieving this unity in the poem; it defines the specific intent of each of the three sections. The initial passage, as we have seen, introduces the philosophical premises of the poem, as well as the major problem to be resolved. The central section, however, drops from the level of meditation to that of debate. The third and final passage once more elevates the discourse by its direct assault on the moral behavior of man. The possibility of an intentional shift from the second to the third sections—a change of voice from Nature to the poet as Professor Arms has asserted—seems dubious from the available evidence; but the shift is, nevertheless, a radical and important one.[20] The appeal of the *reasons* is primarily to the logical faculties and that of the *uses* is principally to the emotions.

The polemic nature of the former appeal is self-evident. The first three lines explicitly state the two points to be debated: the community of the dead and the dignity of natural death—"Yet not to thine eternal resting-place/Shalt thou retire alone, nor couldst thou wish/Couch more magnificent." The community of the dead, an answer to man's fear of the "narrow house," is made clear by a catalogue of past members of the race who have succumbed, a reference to contemporary beings who will share this fate, and a reminder that even future generations "Shall one by one be gathered to thy side,/By those, who in their turn shall follow them." The dignity of natural death is asserted as an answer to the humiliation which a gentleman and humanist must feel being "a brother to the insensible rock/And to the sluggish clod, which the rude swain/Turns with his share, and treads upon." The consolations for this indignity, as offered by the "still voice," are persuasive. The persons who have gone before are men of virtue and social station: "The powerful of the earth—the wise, the good." And furthermore, all the physical forms in Nature lend beauty and dignity to the grave. The earth, the sea, the planets "Are but the solemn decorations all/Of the great tomb of man." Thus, beneath the swelling cadences of the verse and behind the moving imagery of this central passage lies the firm groundwork of a developed argument.

On the other hand, the concluding passage with its pervasive sibilance and its sepia vision of caravans, silent halls, and draped couches contains little that can be restated on the prose level. Man is enjoined to approach his grave "sustained and soothed/ By an unfaltering trust," but he is given no reason to do so— because there is no *reason*. Just as the active and conscious mind accepts sleep, so should it submit to a final relaxation. Only the gauche intellect, anxious in the midst of the Nature which has produced and nurtured him, would ask "Why?" If the consolations for his sense of isolation and for the prick to his intellectual pride have not sufficed, there is little more to be said. For his own purposes the poet had settled the problem of consciousness and its passing, and out of this he had made his master poem.

VII *Other Poems of Death*

The hard-won depth and complexity of "Thanatopsis" was a *tour de force* for Bryant, an achievement that he was unable to sustain or repeat. A piece titled "The Burial-Place" and subtitled "A Fragment" attempts to develop one of the ideas in "Thanatopsis," but it fails to recognize either the dialogue of man with Nature or the resistance of the intellect to death. "The Burial Place"—composed in Great Barrington in 1818 but not collected until the 1832 edition of the poems—is basically a descriptive sketch. It contrasts the yew-studded, willow-shaded cemeteries of England with the harsh purity of the Yankee burial grounds. Unlike Robert Lowell, who could catch the spirit of Promethean heroism in the graveyard of the seafaring folk of Nantucket, Bryant was to see only "melancholy ranks of monuments . . . where the coarse grass, between,/Shoots up its dull

green spikes. . . ." But, as "Thanatopsis" had also pointed out,
Nature supplies its own beauty to the graves of mankind:

> Nature, rebuking the neglect of man,
> Plants often, by the ancient mossy stone,
> The brier-rose, and upon the broken turf
> That clothes the fresher grave, the strawberry plant
> Sprinkles its swell with blossoms, and lays forth
> Her ruddy, pouting fruit. . . .[21]

Sympathy for old-world customs was not, of course, characteristic of Bryant. So similar was the description of the English
rural burial-place to a passage in Irving's *Sketchbook*, that
Bryant felt called upon in the 1832 edition to disclaim any
borrowing from that source.

A subsequent poem, "The Two Graves" (1826), takes up another idea from "Thanatopsis," the notion that death is lonely.
Whereas "Thanatopsis" had argued that the dead join with
others of the race, "The Two Graves" suggests the essential desirability of privacy in death. This reflection is inspired by
the poet's recollection of the graves of an old pioneer couple
who had been buried near their homestead. On returning to
the spot, however, he must come to terms with oblivion:

> Two low green hillocks, two small gray stones,
> Rose over the place that held their bones;
> But the grassy hillocks are levelled again,
> And the keenest eye might search in vain,
> 'Mong briers, and ferns, and paths of sheep,
> For the spot where the aged couple sleep.[22]

This oblivion is not to be lamented. In fact, it is preferable to
a common burial ground where the dead are "Crowded, like
guests in a banquet-room." The old couple have been permitted
to remain near their earthly domicile instead of being "borne
to a distant sphere," and the poet fancies that they still linger
near the spot, quietly enjoying the sunshine, the music of the
brook, and the passing of the seasons. Such sentimental
naturalism, quite different from the philosophy of "Thanatopsis,"
leads the poet to generalize glibly upon the doctrine of the
ascension of the soul after death: "Tis a cruel creed, believe it
not!/Death to the good is a milder lot."

In "The Two Graves," Bryant lapsed back into the poetic pitfalls that he had skillfully avoided in "Thanatopsis": the easy acceptance of Nature as pure benevolence, the unconsidered reliance upon sense experience, the imputation of ethical judgments to death, and the attempt to face the problem of immortality within the framework of Nature poetry. The plight of the conscious mind as it contemplates the immediacy of death has been all but forgotten. The emotional and intellectual power that had created "Thanatopsis" had been, in a few short years, dissipated and eventually lost.

The poet, if he sticks to his craft, may postpone important considerations and turn to other subject matter, but permanently dispel them he cannot. In his declining years, mellowed by success and by failure, sobered by the great public events of his time, and confirmed in his world view, Bryant returned to his theme. Such poems of wisdom as "Among the Trees," "October, 1866," "Tree-Burial," "A Life Time," and "The Flood of Years" lack the lyrical nerve and the intellectual bones of "Thanatopsis"; but each seriously considers the meaning of death for the mortal man.

Within the great cycles of history and nature, these poems assert, death operates unfailingly, not as a curse or a judgment, but as evidence of the permanent reality—spiritual and moral—that lie behind the facade of the moment. "Among the Trees" praises the trees as emblems of the permanence of nature which outlives "The flitting generations of mankind."[23] "October, 1866" is an elegy on the poet's wife, three months deceased, in which his sorrow and grief are gradually transcended through a moral awareness of her continuing influence on his life. "Tree-Burial" presents, sympathetically and sanely, the lament of the Indian mother for her child, and it again dwells upon the close ties which bind the living and the dead.

"A Lifetime" picks up the theme once more as the poet—reflecting upon his wife, his youngest child, and the other loved ones who have died—sees their faces above him "In the far blue deeps of air": "And I stretch my arms with transport/From where I stand below." Still he is enough of a moral man to refrain from an overt wish for union with the dead; the vision fades and he is left alone once more:

> I am gazing into the twilight
>> Where the dim-seen meadows lie,
> And the wind of night is swaying
>> The trees with a heavy sigh.[24]

Finally, in "The Flood of Years" these themes are brought together, and the transience of mortal grief is placed in bold relief against the "eternal Change" and "everlasting Concord." The poem concludes with the reuniting of families and loved ones:

> Old sorrows are forgotten now,
> Or but remembered to make sweet the hour
> That overpays them; wounded hearts that bled
> Or broke are healed forever. In the room
> Of this grief-shadowed present, there shall be
> A Present in whose reign no grief shall gnaw
> The heart . . .[25]

Although there is no longer a sense of conflict and discovery and although the verse of these poems tends toward prolixity, the basic insight into the momentary and partial response to experience by rational men still prevails. The qualities of "Thanatopsis" are distinguishable once more in these poems.

CHAPTER *4*

Poems of Progress

NEARLY ONE FIFTH of the poems composed by William Cullen Bryant make reference, if only in passing, to political ideas or events. This fact, together with his active career as a journalist, has led many to view him as a sort of poet-publicist—as a commentator on public affairs in verse in the tradition of Phillip Freneau and the Connecticut Wits. The very topicality of such titles as "The Embargo," "The Greek Boy," "The Massacre at Scio," and "The Death of Lincoln" has encouraged this generalization to the point where it threatens to obliterate another very important facet of his work. For not only did Bryant master the medium of public verse, but he also wrote creatively and searchingly on the issues which his century brought before him. In his best works he became the seeker after truth, the reconciler of contradictions, the entertainer of doubts and ambiguities. To a lesser extent, perhaps, than in his poems on Nature or death, his poems of progress still reveal the responses of the private self to the experience of the world. The powerful visions which he had of human history and of natural processes are brought forward to make their comments on the "issues" before him and to contribute toward these integrated and balanced complexes of feelings and ideas that are works of art.

When considered in the light of Bryant's career and personal inclinations, the themes of the political verse are predictable: freedom, the rights of mankind, the nobility of the human spirit, human progress. In this respect the poems differ little from his editorials or his public addresses. Though the editorials are deductive, working rapidly toward specifics from an unexamined premise, and the poems tend to be inductive, starting with an image or an experience and culminating with a general idea, in each form of expression the ideological framework is that of the rationalist and liberal. Even in moments of doubt and confusion, the ideals of the early republic still prompted him. Somehow, evidence and experience to the contrary, reasonable men could stand in the center of their environment and direct it toward some higher good. Somehow—all violence, tyranny, greed, and corruption notwithstanding—human society could share with natural processes the propensity to renew itself and to bring forth fresh, beautiful forms of life.

I *The Publicist*

This similarity in the structure of Bryant's thought in the poems and editorials makes necessary some understanding of the man as publicist and as editor-in-chief of the *Evening Post*. For continuing commentary on the political and social affairs of the day, newspaper writing, much more than poetry, provided the better vantage point and commanded the wider audience. Considering Bryant's aversion to the rough-and-tumble of active politics, the editorial chair was indeed a favorable location for him.

This is not to say that he found newspaper work consistently attractive and agreeable. His personal letters gave voice to minor complaints of pressure, fatigue, and boredom, but the most telling statements upon journalism are those made publicly. The first, which is high-minded and innocent, is from an early essay recorded by Nevins in his book about the *Post*; the second, the somber and disillusioned one, appeared in 1851 on the twenty-fifth anniversary of Bryant's connection with the daily:

Circa 1830—

Yet the vocation of a newspaper editor is a useful and indispensable, and if rightly exercised, a noble vocation. It possesses this essential element of dignity—that they who are engaged in it are occupied with questions of the highest importance to the happiness of mankind.[1]

.   .   .   .

November, 1851—

[Journalism] fills the mind with a variety of knowledge relating to the events of the day, but that knowledge is apt to be superficial, since the necessity of attending to many subjects prevents the journalist from thoroughly investigating any. In this way it begets desultory habits of thought, disposing the mind to be satisfied with mere glances at difficult questions, and to dwell only upon plausible commonplaces. The style gains by it in clearness and fluency, but it is apt to become, in consequence of much and hasty writing, loose, diffuse, and stuffed with local barbarisms and cant phrases of the day.[2]

This same essay of 1851, "Reminiscences of the 'Evening Post'," made the point that journalism supplies insights into dark and selfish motives, while it also reveals the "influences" at work in forming public attitudes. Such insight, Bryant explained, creates the temptation "to betray the cause of truth to public opinion," but fortunately the *Evening Post* "has not often yielded."[3] As Mr. Nevins' study of the *Post* demonstrates, this boast and the following one by Bryant were both fully warranted:

Its success and its limits to its success may both, perhaps, be owing to the unaccommodating and insubservient quality. It is often called upon, by a sense of duty, to oppose itself to the general feeling of those from whom a commercial paper must receive its support; it never hesitates to do so. It sometimes finds a powerful member of the community occupied with projects which it deems mischievous; it puts itself in his way, and frustrates his designs, if possible.[4]

II *Liberalism*

Such a conception of the role of the journalist goes far in illuminating the attitudes which Bryant, in association with other members of the editorial board of the *Post*, expressed toward the issues of the era. Motivated by that "sense of duty" which he mentions, the editorial writer speaks for the public as opposed to the private interest; and, through his attack on inequities, he hopes to maintain a stable, democratic social order. A curious negativism in Bryant's position upon many of the great matters which concerned him arises out of his assumption that progress is on the side of mankind and flourishes best when events are allowed to flow without obstruction. His reading in his young manhood in the political economists—Smith,

Say, Thornton, and Ricardo—had confirmed in him his conception of the healthy society as one in which the unregulated flow of goods and payments seeks its proper state of equilibrium. What in the economic sphere was the posture of laissez-faire became in matters of primarily social import a militant desire for freedom and a distrust of artificial restraints.

Even in the decade of Reconstruction, Bryant was able to recollect the events he had witnessed and to discern the signs of continuing improvement in the state of mankind—not because of arbitrary systems or through the intervention of government, but through a kind of enlargement of the sensibilities of men within a relatively free and fluid environment:

> I have lived long, as it may seem to most people, however short the term appears to me when I look back upon it. In that period have occurred various most important changes, both political and social, and on the whole I am rejoiced to say that they have, as I think, improved the condition of mankind. The people of civilized countries have become more enlightened, and enjoy a greater degree of freedom. They have become especially more humane and sympathetic, more disposed to alleviate each other's sufferings. This is the age of charity. In our day, charity has taken forms unknown to former ages, and occupied itself with the cure of evils which former ages neglected.[5]

This social philosophy, which would find one kind of articulation in the poetry, also provided definite "principles" available to the besieged writers of editorials. As he would break down the tariff barriers, so would he oppose the creation of mercantile monopolies. As he would support the rights of labor to bargain for wages, so would he argue for freedom of the press. In matters where the power of the Federal government threatened to create inequities among social classes or sections of the nation—such as through the establishment of the national bank, internal improvements, or in the regulation of currency—his position was that of the strict constructionist of the constitution who advocated severe limitations upon the powers of the Federal government. At each point he would resist control by the few in favor of charity toward the many.

In all of those areas, as Godwin observed, Bryant was more

practical than doctrinaire. While the notion of an open society colored all of his pronouncements, there was no attempt to impose Utopian ideals upon the existing community. Although Godwin might flirt with Fourierism and back the enterprise of the Transcendentalists at Brook Farm and although Leggett— during his short-lived tenure as editor in Bryant's absence— was to wage an immoderate assault on the commercial establishment of New York City, Bryant's strength lay in his willingness to accept the restraints of meliorism. To Emerson, he appeared to be a "historical" democrat, who was "interested in dead or organized, but not in organizing liberty."[6] Among the radicals, his acceptance of social norms seemed at times like conservatism, just as his liberal attitude toward the adjustment of the norms for the public good seemed like radicalism to the Whigs. But through all factional disputes he remained aloof, tending to keep the *Post* as free as possible from the extremes of both radicalism and reaction.

In regard to slavery, the topic of greatest controversy in his day, his position clung closely to liberal principles even while he faced the complexities of crises. When Garrison's *Liberator* brought the attention of the nation to Abolition in 1832, the *Post* was silent; but Bryant had expressed as early as 1820 his hostility toward slavery. Bryant and his editors, consistent with the liberal view, imagined that slavery was doomed to extinction because of its anomalous place in a democratic society. But the wave of reaction instigated by the alliance of Southern slave holders and Northern merchants—the censorship of the mails; the martyrdom of Lovejoy; the move to annex Texas as a nucleus for a slave-holding empire in the West; and, ultimately, those twin horrors, the Fugitive Slave Law and the Missouri Compromise—all of these were clearly anathema to the proponent of a free society. While rival New York newspapers joined with the Washington *Globe* in denouncing the *Post,* Bryant supported the right of the Abolitionists to be heard: "We are resolved that the subject of slavery shall be, as it ever has been, as free a subject for discussion, as the difference between whiggism and democracy, or the differences between Arminians and Calvinists."[7] Such was the position which distinguished the *Post* from the *Emancipator,* which made Bryant a Free Soiler and, later, a Republican, rather than an Abolitionist.

Indeed, it was the moderate position of the *Post*, its opposition to any extension of slavery into the territories but its acquiescence in the predicted demise of the "peculiar institution" through natural causes where it then existed, that formed the rallying point for the Republican Party. Only when secession was an unavoidable fact did Bryant advocate the exertion of Federal power; but once Fort Sumter had been bombarded, he fully recognized the necessity for the preservation of the Union at all costs. His criticism of Lincoln's administration was directed only toward inefficiency and ineffectiveness in military affairs; with the objects of the war, he was in firm agreement.

In other areas also the same staunch regard for principle, mixed with a healthy concern for expeditious action, was characteristic of the *Post* under Bryant's leadership. He backed reform efforts for the creation of a more humane penal system, for the abolition of capital punishment, and for the strengthening of laws regarding criminal carelessness and manslaughter. To the problem of corruption, which had overtaken the many branches of the government during the Civil War, Bryant and Godwin brought a vigorous campaign for civil service reform. Closer to Bryant's personal interests, but less successful as a crusade, was the program for an international copyright. In the 1820's he had formed a common cause on this issue with Benjamin Coleman, the founder of the *Post*; and, in the 1840's, he was to report in detail the acid comments of Charles Dickens on this topic during his American tour. At many levels of social and governmental activity, in great matters and small, Bryant raised the persuasive voice of reason: arguing for equity and justice even while maintaining a wary eye toward what he considered to be dangerous concentrations of power.

Bryant realized, as every experienced publicist must, that the ambiguities and inconsistencies of his position were best left unexamined. To suggest that human reason could offer less than perfect solutions to problems essentially insolvable, or to imply that power itself, in spite of its oppressive and injurious features, was the agent of human progress would be to shake the foundations of the editorial appeal for action. For it was toward results—the crystallization of public opinion, agitation, legislation—that Bryant's prose pieces were directed. To the poems were left speculations, questions, and the incompleted cycles of thought. Thus, to the poems were delegated the loose ends and the unclassified images inappropriate for concentrated appeals on the editorial page.

III *The Public Voice*

Before assuming his role as publicist, Bryant had tested the possibilities of combining the critical and poetic functions. Both "The Embargo" (1808) and "The Ages" (1821) represent trials of this sort, and both illustrate the weaknesses inherent in such a combination. As documents for the historian of culture, they are very valuable, yielding insights into the body of opinion which brought New England to the brink of secession in the Hartford Convention of 1814 and the subsequent relaxation of the Federalists in the "Era of Good Feeling." They are less useful, however, as profiles of the poet's thought. Even though the key problems occur in these poems and initiate important lines of development, their treatment is conventional and pedestrian. They are poems in the public voice which make the concessions necessary to unified opinions, and only in occasional lines does the inward voice dare to suggest its presence.

"The Embargo" was the juvenile satire in which Dr. Peter Bryant had taken such an active interest. It expressed the horror and bitterness of the commercial aristocracy of New England, who watched the decline of the mercantile economy brought about—so they supposed—by Jefferson's decree prohibiting further trade with Great Britain. The poem was cast in the mold of the epideictic verse which had flourished during the Revolution and which had reached its highest point of development in the work of Dwight, Trumbull, and the other Connecticut Wits. Structured on the models of classical rhetoric, "The Embargo," like its predecessors, moves through the formal divisions of the exordium, the narration, the proof, the disproof, and the peroration.[8] Consistent also with the genre was the immoderate abuse of the scoundrel, Jefferson, and the exalted praise of Washington as the just and reasonable man. Though its bellicose tone and melodramatic imagery would have led the mature Bryant, even if he had retained his Federalist sympathies, to repudiate "The Embargo," in 1808 it was a considerable achievement for a prospective poet, and it brought him the approval of his father's friends as well as kind words from a reviewer in the *Monthly Anthology.*

The central argument of this poem, submerged as it is at times through the two hundred and forty-five lines, is of some interest in the light of Bryant's later concerns. His proposition is stated in the following lines, which can also serve as an illustration of the rhetoric and tone of the public voice:

> Oh, ye bright pair, the blessing of mankind!
> Whom time has sanction'd, and whom fate has join'd,
> COMMERCE, that bears the trident of the main,
> And AGRICULTURE, empress of the plain;
> Who, hand in hand, and heav'n-directed, go
> Diffusing gladness through the world below;
> Whoe'er the wretch, would hurl the flaming brand,
> Of dire disunion, palsied be his hand!
> Like 'Cromwell damn'd to everlasting fame,'
> Let unborn ages execrate his name!
> Dark is the scene, yet darker prospects threat,
> And ills may follow unexperienc'd yet!
> Oh Heaven! defend, as future seasons roll,
> This western world from Buonoparte's control,
> Preserve our *Freedom,* and our rights secure,
> While truth subsists, and virtue shall endure![9]

The harmonious functioning of Commerce and Agriculture under the direction of heaven was threatened, so runs the young Bryant's thought, because of the divisive action of the un-principled chief executive. Jefferson's intrusion into the natural workings of the economy, moreover, foreshadows even worse threats to freedom. In the Federalist imagination, the spec-ter of Napoleonic tyranny loomed large; and Bryant rattles its chains frequently and loudly. For his efforts to maintain peace with Napoleon and for the purchase of the Louisiana Territory, Jefferson is caricatured as "the *willing vassal* of imperious France." For his appeal for support to the democratic masses, Jefferson is described as a "supple" demagogue who lies and flatters in order to secure "each blockhead's vote."

The poem has its happier sentiments, however; for, once "the deep laid plot" is uncovered and the "pirate Gaul" repelled, a new era is in the offing with prosperity for both merchant and yeoman. In the following lines, prophesying the cheerful future, appears the first hint of the idea of progress in Bryant's verse:

> Then on safe seas the merchant's barque shall fly,
> Our waving flag shall kiss the polar sky;
> On canvas wings our thunders shall be borne,
> Far to the west, or tow'rd the rising morn;
> Then may we dare a haughty tyrant's rage,
> And gain the blessings of an unborn age.
>
> 'Tis done, behold the cheerful prospects rise!
> And splendid scenes the startled eye surprise;
> Lo! busy commerce courts the prosperous main;
> And peace and plenty glad our shores again!
> Th' industrious swain sees nature smile around
> His fields with fruit, with flocks, his pastures crown'd.

But though the communal idea is portrayed in vivid colors, in only one short passage of the peroration does the voice of the boy—sensitive to natural imagery and ambitious to prove himself among men—express itself, and then indirectly, in a figure intended to describe the outgrowth of a new nation from the old:

> Thus in a fallen tree, from sprouting roots,
> With sudden growth, a tender sapling shoots,
> Improves from day to day, delights the eyes
> With strength and beauty, stateliness and size,
> Puts forth robuster arms, and broader leaves,
> And high in air, its branching head upheaves.

If the doctrine of progess is only implicit in "The Embargo," obscured, as it were, behind partisan sword-rattling and neo-Classical drapery, in "The Ages" (1821) the concept becomes offensively explicit. Although "The Ages" was not issued in pamphlet form, as "The Embargo" had been, in order to disseminate a particular political viewpoint, it is, nonetheless, as carefully directed toward a particular audience and as much a vehicle of communal belief as "The Embargo" itself. Its delivery at the Harvard Commencement of 1821, its subsequent publication in Cambridge by Hillard and Metcalf, and its wide, if not enthusiastic, acceptance by the public as a significant production by the leading American poet are all signs of the poem's limitations as well as indications of its strength.

A piece of illuminating correspondence regarding Bryant's composition of the poem, unearthed and analyzed by Professor Glicksberg, tends to confirm the impression of the poem received by the reader. The problem, as seen by Bryant's correspondent, was whether to deliver a classical or a pathetic oration—that is, whether the audience should be stirred largely by the weight of accumulated rational argument or by a direct appeal to the sensibilities. But, the advice ran on to say, matters of political concern were best avoided.[10] The stricture was timely; and Bryant, in deference to the Era of Good Feeling, carefully refrained from commentary on the contemporary political scene. That his composition combined both classical and pathetic elements, leaning toward the pathetic, was, however, less significant than that this would be the last time he would compose a lengthy poem to suit the public temper on a particular occasion.

Although the bland optimism of the poem should have been inescapable for any reader, all editions of the work were accompanied by a note which describes its contents and explains its simple purpose: "In this poem, written and first printed in the year 1821, the author has endeavored, from a survey of the past ages of the world, and of the successive advances of mankind in knowledge, virtue, and happiness, to justify and confirm the hopes of the philanthropist for the future destinies of the human race."[11]

What is omitted from this statement about the poem's message is that the philanthropist must look toward the continental United States for the realization of his "hopes." The provincialism of the poem is inescapable, from the Unitarian references to Christ ("The light of hope, the leading star of love,"), through the rejection of the medieval church ("Horrible forms of worship, that, of old/Held, o'er the shuddering realms, unquestioned sway"), to the celebration of Boston harbor ("yon bright blue bay," where "Lifts the white throng of sails, that bear or bring/The commerce of the world").

The basis for the poet's optimism is the growth of human liberty, made possible by the new natural environment of the North American continent. That the human personality has its own inherent determinisms, as Edwards had recognized in his polemic on *Free Will*, or that the natural order imposes a discipline upon all human action, as Emerson was to proclaim in his essay, *Fate*, were considerations easily overlooked in Bryant's paean to freedom. In the concluding three stanzas he uses the image of the fetter, or shackles, to suggest the quality of liberty which he has in mind—the release from bondage of the prisoner or slave:

> Here the free spirit of mankind, at length,
> Throws its last fetters off; and who shall place
> A limit to the giant's unchained strength,
> Or curb his swiftness in the forward race?
> On, like the comet's way through infinite space,
> Stretches the long untravelled path of light,
> Into the depths of ages; we may trace,
> Afar, the brightening glory of its flight,
> Till the receding rays are lost to human sight.[12]

In spite of her gloomy history of oppression, Europe, too, has hope:

> Europe is given a prey to sterner fates,
> And writhes in shackles; strong the arms that chain
> To earth her struggling multitude of states;
> She too is strong, and might not chafe in vain
> Against them . . .
> . . . the moment set
> To rescue and raise up, draws near—but is not yet.

But Americans have only the "fetters" of abundance, and the wildness of nature provides an ample shield against aggression:

> But thou, my country, thou shalt never fall,
> Save with thy children—thy maternal care,
> Thy lavish love, thy blessings showered on all—
> These are thy fetters—seas and stormy air
> Are the wide barrier of thy borders, where,
> Among thy gallant sons who guard thee well,
> Thou laugh'st at enemies: who shall then declare
> The date of thy deep-founded strength, or tell
> How happy, in thy lap, the sons of men shall dwell?

Conventional as it is, this image of the "fetters" transmits its quota of feeling and idea. For a nation with the memory of revolution still as vivid as the stench of gunpowder, no further development of the notion was necessary. The ringing indictment of tyranny contained in the Declaration of Independence is implicit in each line of such a poem as "The Ages," and the critic who would seek the depths of its meaning should turn to the militant oratory of the later decades of the eighteenth century. Though Bryant was not deeply involved in his theme—indeed, he wrote a friend that composing this poem had made him "sick"—he understood his audience well.[13] His measured rhetoric, his appeals to the pathetic impulses, and his descriptive vagueness—all these meet the purposes of the occasion.

The generation which he addressed, those Harvard graduates of 1821, were of the *epigoni*, arriving too late on the scene of history to play heroic roles in either of the two wars against Great Britain. For Ralph Waldo Emerson, as for other young men in that audience, the problem of the past was crucial indeed. And if Emerson's major theme in his early works was "The sun shines today also," this was not to deny the urgency of Bryant's vision of the progress of freedom but only to reassert it with a new emphasis. Emerson no less than Bryant invoked the spirit of freedom and found its epitome in the development of the American republic. His appeal went further and deeper than Bryant's, of course, for Emerson searched out the hidden resources of intellect and spirit in democratic man; but the motivation was directed by the same general cultural predicament. The old cries of "Liberty," which had once been calls to the standard, had to be translated into a social philosophy of reform rather than of revolution, one of creative thought rather than of violent action. Thus, in a sense, what "Nature" and "The American Scholar" were to the generation of the late 1830's, "The Ages" was to that of the early 1820's.

IV *Poems of Revolution*

Bryant was to abandon this type of massive statement upon his removal to New York, and the poems of the 1820's with political implications tend to be sharper in focus and more explicit in their sympathies. Like many Americans, Bryant was deeply stirred by the conflict in Greece. The situation of the Greek patriots who were attempting to rid their homeland of the Turkish oppressors was too similar to that of the Minutemen of '76 to be overlooked, and the signs suggested that the forces of Liberty were at work once more. Bryant's contribution to public sentiment was largely poetic (he was editing quarterlies and had not yet joined the *Post*), and it consisted of several lyrical profiles of the Greek heroes.

Representative of these poems, though perhaps more subtle than "The Greek Amazon" (1824), or "The Greek Partisan" (1825), was "The Greek Boy" (1826, 1827). The boy, Evangelides, was an actual public figure in New York at the time. The press had given him considerable publicity, and his likeness was painted in oils by the prominent artist, Robert E. Weir. Subsequently engraved, this portrait, accompanied by Bryant's poem, appeared in *The Talisman* of 1826. The portrait tries to suggest the heritage of the classical past as it lingers in the boy's calm features, and the poem, explicit in its praise for his "martial form," finds hope for the future in one whose "ears have drunk the woodland strains/Heard by old poets." Evangelides was, for Bryant, a symbol of the regenerative forces at work in society; and the final stanza projects upon Greece that optimism of "The Ages" that had bathed America in its warm glow:

> Now is thy nation free, though late;
> Thy elder brethren broke—
> Broke, ere thy spirit felt its weight—
> The intolerable yoke.
> And Greece, decayed, dethroned, doth see
> Her youth renewed in such as thee:
> A shoot of that old vine that made
> The nations silent in its shade.[14]

Yet there was a difference between telling the gallant sons of Harvard graduating in 1821 to laugh at their enemies and encouraging Greek partisans to shed blood for the cause of freedom. This difference emerges as the central theme of "The Conjunction of Venus and Jupiter" (1826) as the poet reflects on the portents for America, and then for Greece, of the approach of these two planets to one another:

Emblems of power and beauty! well may they
Shine brightest on our borders, and withdraw
Toward the great Pacific, marking out
The path of empire. . . .

. . . .

. . . Happy days to them
That wed this evening!—a long life of love,
And blooming sons and daughters! Happy they
Born at this hour, for they shall see an age
Whiter and holier than the past, and go
Late to their graves. Men shall wear softer hearts,
And shudder at the butcheries of war,
As now at other murders.

. . . Hapless Greece!
Enough of blood has wet thy rocks, and stained
Thy rivers. . .

. . . .

. . . In yonder mingling lights
There is an omen of good days for thee.
Thou shalt arise from midst the dust and sit
Again among the nations. Thine own arm
Shall yet redeem thee.[15]

Certainly the emblems of power and beauty are brightest
in the happy land of America, but are they really omens for
Greece? Does the power of Jupiter really apply to the kind of
strength needed to fight a successful rebellion, or does the beauty
of Venus correspond to the terror and bitterness which motivate
men to fight for a new social order? While the conjunction of
the two planets may prompt a conceit which describes America's
"path of empire," there is nothing in the poem to explain how
the liaison between these Roman deities can give "new strength"
to the embattled Greek partisans.

Thus, the poet's limitation becomes embarrassingly evident.
Although the heroic gesture was for Bryant a literary commonplace and though he had fought by the sides of Achilles and
Aeneus, the realities of rebellion were unfamiliar to him. When
he promises that "And God and thy good sword shall yet work

out,/For thee, a terrible deliverance," it is the conventional rhetoric of the public voice still speaking.

Indeed, in a poem like "To the Apennines" (1835) he envisions the spirit of freedom as something totally removed from the ordinary political trials of men. Turning once more to Nature, Bryant finds in the lofty mountains the symbol for his idealistic conception of liberty:

> In [the Apennines] the heart that sighs for freedom seeks
>   Her image; there the winds no barrier know,
> Clouds come and rest and leave your fairy peaks;
>   While even the immaterial Mind, below,
> And Thought, her wingèd offspring, chained by power,
> Pine silently for the redeeming hour.[16]

That the citizens of the Italian states—betrayed, as it seemed to many, by the Congress of Vienna, and even then fermenting with the revolutionary violence which was to lead to eventual reunification—should look to the Apennines as some distant "image" of freedom is both plausible and poetically effective. But the disturbing union in this symbol of beauty and power is still unresolved. The explicit contrast in the poem between the "eternal Peace" of the Apennines and the futile, vicious struggles of the plains below in no way contributes to an understanding of how ideals can become operative within public life. The private voice, however, had at last spoken out, if only to find a greater peace than society can offer.

V *"The Fountain"*

The drift toward a mature political verse had begun, and in "The Fountain" (1839) Bryant boldly combined his vision of Nature and his conception of human progress. Something of the "happy land" lingers in his description of the agrarian society which evolves by the "fountain" (a woodland spring), but far mightier forces are at work in the poem than those which make and overthrow mere empires. No longer is the rise of a national republic central to the cosmic enterprise, for framing the poem is a terrifying conception of the mysterious subterranean forces which have created the spring and which

shall, in the due course of time, destroy it. The optimism of
Bryant's early faith in human progress is thus drastically
qualified by the discovery of geological change.

"The Fountain" is a complex poem, and the symbolic use
of the fountain—both as a structural device and as a means for
synthesizing ideas—is one of Bryant's finest achievements. Starting with a simple and prosaic analogy between the emergence
of clear, cool water from "red mould and slimy roots of earth"
and the mysterious ways of God, who brings "from the dark
and foul, the pure and bright," the poet moves quickly into
his personal response to the fountain. His observation of the
wild-vine, the spice-bush, the viburnum, and the chipping
sparrow conjures up scenes from the long history of the fountain: first before the intrusion of man, and then the "histories
that stir the heart/With deeper feeling," the days of barbarism,
savage warfare, and hunting. From these dark ages—the poem
is rich in the imagery of color and light—rise the pure and
bright waters of an agricultural society:

> . . . White cottages were seen
> With rose-trees at the windows; barns from which
> Came loud and shrill the crowing of the cock;
> Pastures where rolled and neighed the lordly horse,
> And white flocks browsed and bleated.[17]

With the ascent of civilization, however, the fountain—like
Nature itself—becomes less significant to the surrounding life.
Eventually it is merely an isolated watering spot for the less
established members of the community—the woodsman, the
hunter, the soldier—and a place for children to play. Here, too,
the unsophisticated couples come:

> . . . At eve,
> When thou wert crimson with the crimson sky,
> Lovers have gazed upon thee, and have thought
> Their mingled lives should flow as peacefully
> And brightly as thy waters.

But here also comes the philosopher to read the great truth,
not of human progress, but of "eternal change" within the
"eternal order" of the universe:

[100]

> . . . Here the sage,
> Gazing into thy self-replenished depth,
> Has seen eternal order circumscribe
> And bound the motions of eternal change,
> And from the gushing of thy simple fount
> Has reasoned to the mighty universe.

This "eternal change" which the poet, as well as the sage, recognized, destroys even as it creates. Although no mention is made of the future for the secure rural community which had grown up near the spring, the concluding lines cryptically imply a dark prophecy. Just as the dynamic processes which had brought clear water out of the bowels of the earth had also given rise to a higher state of culture, so these same processes, which can choke off the water at its source or pollute it in passage, can also demolish the "happy land." This conclusion is left unstated, and the conjectures of the poet are intentionally tentative. The poem's message of doom is muted, and these concluding lines are only a solemn reminder of the natural limits of human progress:

> Is there no other change for thee, that lurks
> Among the future ages? Will not man
> Seek out strange arts to wither and deform
> The pleasant landscape which thou makest green?
> Or shall the veins that feed thy constant stream
> Be choked in middle earth, and flow no more
> For ever, that the water-plants along
> Thy channel perish, and the bird in vain
> Alight to drink? Haply shall these green hills
> Sink, with the lapse of years, into the gulf
> Of ocean waters, and thy source be lost
> Amidst the bitter brine? Or shall they rise,
> Upheaved in broken cliffs and airy peaks,
> Haunts of the eagle and the snake, and thou
> Gush midway from the bare and barren steep?

This conception of geologic change—in which no apparent purpose is operative but only immutable and inflexible natural laws—was probably derived, as Professor Ringe has pointed out, from Bryant's reading in *The Principles of Geology* by Sir Charles Lyell.[18] The controversial theory of uniformitarianism, which had been advanced by Lyell and attacked by the conservative wing of Protestantism, had emphasized the consistency of natural causes from past ages to the present in the formation of the surface of the earth. For biblical scholars, the uniformitarian theory argued against any providential intervention in the familiar catastrophes of flood and fire; and, for the pious laymen, it placed God too far back in the eons of creation.

"The Fountain" is notable for its subtle avoidance of these issues, and for its use of the theory for imaginative rather than for polemical purposes. In a subsequent poem, "A Hymn of the Sea" (1842), Bryant was to assure the public that God, even though He had taken up geology, was still in His Heaven; but "The Fountain" reveals the private processes of imaginative assimilation at work. None of his poems after this period was to sing quite so jauntily of progress, and the ones that took up the theme were to be more restrained in their prophetic glances into the cloudy future.

By his indirection, Bryant confused those readers who shared the unexamined belief in progress which had been defined by "The Ages" and which was assumed by the editorial policy of the *Evening Post*. Parke Godwin's edition of the poems, for example, contains a long note speculating on the place that "The Fountain"—along with "The Evening Revery" and "Noon" (other poems of time and change)—was to fill in a projected, but never completed, work on the settlement of the New World.[19] That Bryant should have achieved a greater depth than that suggested by "a series of pictures connected by a narrative of personal adventures" was beyond Godwin's comprehension. Unintentionally, Bryant had achieved the kind of healthy obscurantism that is the fate of the poet who searches deeply into himself. But not until the composition of "The Antiquity of Freedom" (1842) was he able to make the elements of natural beauty, progress, power, and freedom fully cohesive and articulate within his personal vision.

VI *"The Antiquity of Freedom"*

This master poem, widely read in its own time and frequently anthologized in our own, manages to balance affirmations against reservations and to check the cryptic tendencies of "The

Fountain." In its activism and in its seriousness it represents the matured expression of the poet and the definitive position that he was to take, both personally and publicly, on the problems of social order.

Unlike the other poems of progress, "The Antiquity of Freedom" abandons historical figures and natural objects as unifying devices. Instead, directly out of eighteenth-century verse strides the allegorical figure of "Freedom" ("armed to the teeth"), who contends with other, somewhat theatrical, figures identified as "Power" and "Tyranny." Curiously enough, the cumbersome and archaic quality of the allegory fades under Bryant's warmth and skill; and his purpose of elevating his discourse to a philosophical level, while avoiding topical references, is achieved. The narrative element is reduced to a minimum, the poem is kept fairly brief, and the play of ideas is permitted to dominate the verse.

Both beauty and power are introduced early in the poem. The beauty is that of Nature, and the first twelve lines describe the forest glade in which peace and serenity reside:

> Here are old trees, tall oaks, and gnarlèd pines,
> That stream with gray-green mosses; here the ground
> Was never trenched by spade, and flowers spring up
> Unsown, and die ungathered. It is sweet
> To linger here . . .[20]

The poet is moved by the scene, however, to think "Back to the earliest days of liberty," and immediately he apostrophizes the figure of "Freedom":

> O FREEDOM! thou art not, as poets dream,
> A fair young girl, with light and delicate limbs,
> And wavy tresses gushing from the cap
> With which the Roman master crowned his slave
> When he took off the gyves. A bearded man,
> Armed to the teeth, art thou; one mailèd hand
> Grasps the broad shield, and one the sword; thy brow,
> Glorious in beauty though it be, is scarred
> With tokens of old wars; thy massive limbs
> Are strong with struggling.

This figure of manly strength, of course, though scarred and made strong by trials and experience, has its own "beauty." Through his experiences in the area of public affairs, Bryant had come to terms with the activist creed. No longer the pure and innocent idealist who would dream of freedom as a distant peak or as a fair young maiden, he had come to an acceptance of moral conflict as a principle of political progress. Inadequate, indeed, was a chaste, neo-Classic *Liberté* in the midst of the harsh struggles of the age; and it is even doubtful that Bryant would have accepted the detached colossus on Bedloe's Island as an appropriate symbol for the hard-won freedom which he contemplated.

The poem rings with the noise of battle and bristles with the harsh energy of the ancient warrior. Freedom withstands the bolts of Power; and, when he is imprisoned and bound by the chain of oppression

> The links are shivered, and the prison-walls
> Fall outward; terribly thou springest forth,
> As springs the flame above a burning pile,
> And shoutest to the nations, who return
> Thy shoutings, while the pale oppressor flies.

Thus, it is clear, Power must be met with Freedom's own power; the brutal violence of the sword is inseparable from man's progress toward eventual freedom. Whereas "The Conjunction of Venus and Jupiter" had considered the momentary meeting of these two symbols to be fortuitous, "The Antiquity of Freedom" asserts the perpetual fusion of beauty and power within the guise (or concept) of Freedom. The record of human progress thus becomes not the simple pattern depicted in "The Ages" but an evolution directed by men toward the specific goal of Liberty. The strong affirmation of an activist creed contained in this poem goes far beyond the enthusiasms of the 1820's, and it deepens our understanding of Bryant's later attitudes toward Lincoln and the Civil War.

The poet also clarifies his position on the extent of human responsibility: Freedom is a cause espoused by man, but not created by him: "Thy birthright was not given by human hands:/

Thou wert twin-born with man. . . ." And tyranny, like Evil in the theology of Protestant liberalism, is merely a negation of the Good:

> . . . Tyranny himself,
> Thy enemy, although of reverend look,
> Hoary with many years, and far obeyed,
> Is later born than thou; and as he meets
> The grave defiance of thine elder eye,
> The usurper trembles in his fastnesses.

It is on the problem of tyranny and civilization that all but the last eight lines dwell. In the tradition of the natural-rights philosophy, the pristine innocence of free men is threatened by the growth of civilization with its many forms of restraint. Thus, while Freedom has in times past withstood Power and Tyranny, now he must be warned against "subtler" forms of snares and ambush:

> Quaint maskers, wearing fair and gallant forms
> To catch thy gaze, and uttering graceful words
> To charm thy ear; while his sly imps, by stealth
> Twine round thee threads of steel, light thread on thread,
> That grow to fetters; or bind down thy arms
> With chains concealed in chaplets. Oh! not yet
> Mayst thou unbrace thy corslet, nor lay by
> Thy sword; nor yet, O Freedom! close thy lids,
> In slumber; for thine enemy never sleeps,
> And thou must watch and combat till the day
> Of the new earth and heaven.

That a raging Samson should become a Gulliver bound by Lilliputians is, quite naturally, intolerable. Freedom of the noble brow must—as Bryant well knew—"watch and combat" even in the modern, democratic society to preserve his primal identity.

Such a situation has its heroic qualities, and it is upon these that the peroration dwells, but underneath runs the deeper dye of irony and pathos. Must the aged warrior be constantly awake against "fair and gallant forms"—and even be wary of the very garlands which signify his victory? The concluding lines are directed toward the pathos rather than the irony of Freedom's plight, but the insight into the ambiguities of political theory is present. If Freedom rose from Nature, why should he not, like man, find respite from his constant vigilance in the charming solitudes of the forest?

> . . . But wouldst thou rest
> Awhile from tumult and the frauds of men,
> These old and friendly solitudes invite
> Thy visit. They, while yet the forest-trees
> Were young upon the unviolated earth,
> And yet the moss-stains on the rock were new,
> Beheld thy glorious childhood, and rejoiced.

Like "The Fountain," this poem recognizes the context into which the long fight for human liberty must be placed. The values of activism are real and substantial, but they must also admit to the corrective balance of peace and acquiescence. Within the matured philosophical view, nature and society, contemplation and service, rest and conflict are all elements of the higher order.

VII *Calls to the Standard*

After the publication of *The Fountain and Other Poems* (1842), Bryant wrote no other poems which performed the synthetic function of "The Fountain" or of "The Antiquity of Freedom." The poems in the volume titled *The Little People of the Snow* (1863), as Godwin explains, provided a release for the poet from "the horrors of war" through escapist fantasies.[21] But on the other hand, there were the militant calls to the standard: "O Mother of a Mighty Race" (1846) for the war with Mexico and "Our Country's Call" (1861) for the Civil War. There are also two poems dealing with the progress of freedom in Italy and Spain: the first ("Italy," 1860) praises the courage and determination of the rebellious populace; the second ("A Brighter Day," 1867) laments the triumph of reactionary forces. And finally, there were two poems inculcating loyal Unionists with Bryant's firm sentiments at the close of the Civil War: "The Death of Lincoln" (1865) and "The Death of Slavery" (1866). With the exception of the fantasies, all of these poems are motivated by the activism of "The Antiquity of Freedom." Poetry becomes, even more than it had in "The Ages" and in "The Conjunction of Venus and Jupiter," a vehicle for propaganda. The ideas which once had been probed and doubted become crystallized once more and serve as weapons in the political struggles of the day.

As rallying points for public opinion, the poems about Lincoln and about slavery are models of their kind. The first stanza of the elegy has the indelible force of Lincoln's personality in it, and combines neatly his antithetical virtues of strength and compassion:

> Oh, slow to smite and swift to spare,
> Gentle and merciful and just!
> Who, in the fear of God, didst bear
> Thy sword of power, a nation's trust![22]

And "The Death of Slavery" skillfully, if extravagantly, mobilizes Gothic terror, religious piety, nationalistic fervor, and moralistic sentimentality in denouncing involuntary servitude. In it was the voice of a publicist and orator who no longer sought out the bias of his audience but who strove mightily to direct it to his purposes. In sanctifying the martyred leader, Bryant kept his eye on the mild policies of Lincoln's plans for reconstruction. In celebrating the demise of Negro slavery, Bryant systematically condemned the cowards, hypocrites, and criminals who had defended it and were still potential enemies of freedom.

If the poet in William Cullen Bryant had withered away under the glare of public life, the informed and eager partisan still remained, willing to dedicate his energies, if not to the search for truth, at least to the maintenance of a society in which truth could flourish.

CHAPTER 5

The Divided Voice

IF BRYANT'S VACILLATION between epideictic and contemplative verse in his poems of progress was, on one level, a re-enactment of the age-old dilemma of the personal poet who feels compelled to tithe his talent to the social good, on a more profound level this indecision was symptomatic of the fundamental weakness of his poetry. Bryant was seldom able to speak with the firm, clear, original voice of his own genius. Though he sensed early and rightly that his was the way of the poet, he never truly understood the terms of his vocation. Though his voice in a few great poems rises to uniqueness, the grounds for his triumphs were never clear to him. And though, at times, he brought into the realm of the articulate his personal vision of the universal experience, he seemed unable to sustain his best insights and to profit by his successes.

This basic criticism of Bryant as a poet need not obscure, however, our appreciation of his many accomplishments. Bryant— given his nature and environment—faced an inevitable and nearly unsolvable dilemma. His preternaturally early development, his search for parental approval, the facile action of his mind as it worked backward and forward between experience and introspection, the unquestioned authority of British culture, the fluid state of American letters and criticism during the years of his maturation—all of these militated against the kind of ultimate commitment required of the creative artist. Out of his dilemma he made the best that might have been anticipated. He dignified Nature both as a subject and as a metaphor, he made some of his deeper thoughts available to the masses, he not only expressed himself in the discipline of traditional meters but pioneered also in the use of freer, more natural rhythms.

Yet Bryant could never make the basic decision which

Emerson was to formulate as the choice between self-reliance and conformity. To have fallen back upon his own resources would have meant isolation and obscurity; to have molded himself deliberately on the pattern of an acknowledged poet—Wordsworth or Byron—would have meant the sacrifice of his independence as a Yankee and an American. Either choice would have guaranteed his work a fullness and consistency; either choice would have allowed him to mine his talent more deeply and to understand the dynamics of his creative process. But the choice was not made. His poetic gift broadened—to use Emerson's figure—in concentric circles and not according to any linear directive. As a poet he was an eclectic; as an individual, a pragmatist. Unlike the great modern poets—Yeats, Rilke, Eliot, Stevens—who would build in part upon the failures of their predecessors, Bryant faced the problems of multiplicity and divided purpose with a gift for adaptability rather than with integrity and self-awareness. Lacking within him the tight knot of conviction, he could never fulfill the promise implicit in his vocation.

This pathetic flaw influenced every aspect of his poetry, but it is most noticeable in the two areas with which this chapter will deal: poetic theory and poetic technique. In his infrequent attempts to reflect upon his art, Bryant was never able to formulate an adequate conception of the relationship between poetic ends and poetic means. If, on the one hand, he resisted the mechanical functionalism of the classical rhetoric he had absorbed through his formal education, he also balked at the obvious alternative—a thoroughgoing estheticism. Neither "art for morality's sake" nor "art for art's sake" provided him with a rationale for his own creativity. Thus, his critical fumblings expose only too well his policy of drifting between the neo-Classical Scylla and the Romantic Charybdis.

I *Poetic Theory*

His sole effort at sustained criticism, *The Lectures on Poetry* (1825-26), manfully attempted to declare a position on this issue of ends and means. In the second of the four lectures, entitled "On the Value and Uses of Poetry," he defined the ultimate end of poetry as moral uplift and spiritual refinement.

While admitting that a good deal of poetry is mere "amusement, an agreeable intellectual exercise," Bryant stressed the nobler goals: "[Poetry] has, however, a still higher value when regarded as in some sort the support of our innocence, for there is ever something pure and elevated in the creations of poetry. Its spirit is an aspiration after superhuman beauty and majesty, which, if it has no affinity with, has at least some likeness to virtue."[1]

How are these goals to be reached? Three positive recommendations may be gleaned from the *Lectures*: first, American poetry should tap the rich resources of native speech and natural imagery; second, poetry should profit from the poetic "experiments" of the past rather than strive for novelty; third, poetry should be "suggestive" and not attempt literal representation. Independently, each of these methods could produce an esthetic experience which might be considered ennobling and spiritual. The first—that of tapping native resources—is, indeed, the way that Whitman chose; the second is that of the traditionalist Longfellow; the third approximates the path of mysterious ambiguity by which Poe climbed toward the "supernal." But, in combination, the methods are unstable and too often ineffective. Like the man who believed in all religions in hopes of hitting upon one that was right, Bryant, in his criticism as well as in his poetry, obscured his purpose through the multiplicity of his means. While there is nothing intrinsically wrong about using traditional verse forms to praise American scenery, as Bryant did repeatedly, the total effect of the poem is as much conditioned by the imported stanzaic patterns as it is by the vastness and wildness of the landscape. And in similar fashion the total effect of the poem derives as much from the "suggestive" manner in which the scene is described as it does upon the natural details of physical location. Thus, what Bryant conceived as various roads to the same city were actually variable determinants which could shift the locus of the destination across the surface of a map. Bryant failed to see that the poetic end was absolutely dependent upon the poetic means—that a diversity of means did not simplify but, to the contrary, complicated the creative process.

Particularly in his treatment of the idea of "suggestion" does his theorizing expose his confusion. For Bryant, the "suggestive" power of poetry arose from its capacity to encourage the imagination along "the path which the poet only points out, and shapes its visions from the scenes and allusions which he gives." As a "suggestive art" poetry stands in contrast to the "imitative" arts of painting and sculpture which only reproduce "sensible objects." While these "imitative" arts carefully define reality in its form and substance, poetry utilizes "arbitrary symbols" (language) in order to excite the imagination "most powerfully and delightfully." To Bryant, examples of great poetry which affect the imagination are Milton's portrayals of Eve and of Satan.[2] In each case the imagination feeds upon a few hints in order to visualize the physical and moral qualities of the character. Now, had Bryant been satisfied to expand upon this point, his conception of poetry would have been unified and usable—perhaps even comparable to that put forward by Poe in "The Poetic Principle." But, still suspicious of the currents of unregulated "imagination," he foundered upon the shoals of common sense.

From the point at which Bryant took up in his essay the roles of *emotion* and *intellect* in poetry, the idea of "suggestion" is all but forgotten. Once the door has been opened to "the language of the passions" and to "direct lessons of wisdom," then the sources of imaginative vitality—mystery, wonder, spontaneity—retire to their private chambers. Once the "suggestive" power of poetry becomes comprehensive enough to include the familiar rhetorical devices for kindling emotions and instilling ideas, there is little left in poetry to distinguish it from prose. In fact, such is the conclusion at which Bryant, at the close of his first *Lecture*, sadly and quietly arrives. He admits that the only way in which he can distinguish between poetry and "eloquence" is by metrical arrangement.[3] This conclusion, far removed from the brave premise upon which he had built his critical remarks, is a clear indication of his inability to maintain a consistent understanding of his creative work.

II *Form and Diction*

In Bryant's attitude toward poetic form, as in his theories of poetry, there is a fundamental deficiency. Even a rapid perusal of the collected poetry reveals his constant experimentation with rhyme schemes, stanzaic units, and meter. Although much of his verse is in rhymed quatrains, he adapted easily to the sonnet form, the Spenserian measure, and the ballad. He was adept at both conventional rhyme schemes and improvised patterns. In "To a Waterfowl," for example, he skillfully combines trimeters and pentameters within the rhymed quatrain. "Green River" is a marvelous use of rhymed tetrameter couplets to create a variety of effects. And in a number of poems, "Catterskill Falls" for one, he affixes this rhymed tetrameter couplet as a braking device at the conclusion of each conventional stanza.[4]

Perhaps Bryant can be praised, as Professor McDowell has praised him, for the estimable virtues of versatility and liberality in his use of poetic form. But for the poet such praise is, at best, a kind of honorable mention. With each successive mastery of a form Bryant reaffirms his technical competence but seldom does the novel device stimulate discoveries of fresh ideas or emotions. Too often the experiment suggests that the poet is still straining for the better vehicle, still seeking for the external order of discipline which will bring his work alive. Instead of pressing the more viable forms to the limit of their capacity, he dissipates his strength upon a variety of minor problems. That very breadth and restlessness, which characterized Bryant as a student of Nature and Society and which makes him interesting as a journalist and traveler, tended to produce a body of verse which has more amplitude than depth, more intelligence than conviction.

Nor does Bryant appear to have come to grips with the problem of language. His critical observations usually revolved around two key points. The first is obviously indebted to the viewpoint of Wordsworth, expressed in the "Preface" of *The Lyrical Ballads,* in its appeal for a less stylized and a more natural diction in poetry. Thus the poet—by omitting "stiff Latinisms," "hackneyed phrases," and "the recondite or remote allusion" from his verses—can acquire a "household" or "luminous" style.[5] Bryant praised the tendency of contemporary poets to go "directly to nature for their imagery, instead of taking it from what once had been regarded as the common stock of the guild of poets."[6]

The second point which Bryant made about language in the *Lectures* was that the tongue spoken by Americans and available to the native poet was a successfully transplanted version of a basic Anglo-Saxon. Having the flexibility to meet the new political and scientific conditions of American life, this language still retained the beauty and integrity of its early roots. Bryant summarized his position thus: "It has grown up, as every forcible and beautiful language has done, among a simple and unlettered people; it has accommodated itself, in the first place, to the things of nature, and, as civilization advanced, to the things of art; and thus it has become a language full of picturesque forms of expression, yet fitted for the purposes of science."[7]

Both of these points were to become axiomatic for generations of American writers, not merely because they provided a rationalization for a national literature, but because their implications opened up new and exciting vistas for expression. The downright earthiness of the American vernacular, the latent ironies and humor of dialect, the possibilities of "organic" expression which united matter and idea in a single word or phrase—all of these were to announce those great experiments in language by Whitman, Thoreau, Melville, and Mark Twain. But Bryant failed to sense the implications of his theory. For him the return to Nature for diction meant merely the naming of indigenous plants, birds, and animals in the simple vernacular and the brief, infrequent mention of place names in his poems. For Bryant the historical condition of the transplanted language implied none of the high ironies that ring through the rhetoric of *Moby Dick*; to the contrary, the diction of the poet should abhor "subtilties of thought" and adhere "to the common track of human intelligence."[8]

His confusion over the "suggestive" function of poetry spills over into this area of diction. On the one hand, he explains in the *Lectures* that language, for all its achievements, "is still limited and imperfect, and . . . falls infinitely short of the mighty and diversified world of matter and thought of which it professes to be the representative."[9] And he conceives of the way in which descriptive passages function as "glimpses of things thrown into the mind; here and there a trace of an outline; here a gleam of light, and there a dash of shade."[10] Yet, on the other hand, he could speak of language as "a great machine"[11] and employ—as we have seen in his epideictic verse—all of the mechanical devices for persuasion typical of utilitarian rhetoric. Lacking any theoretical approach to language which did any more than describe the current situation, Bryant was not prepared to formulate an original position for his own work. His poetic diction avoids the more obvious pedantry and artifice of earlier American poets, which he had pointed out in some detail in an essay-review of 1818;[12] yet he retained many vestiges of the former style. And while the notion of "suggestion" brought an imaginative vitality to his better poems, a workable concept was never to emerge from the clouded background evoked by the *Lectures*.

Bryant sought no half-way house in prosody, as he had in poetic diction. Instead, like Wordsworth and the Victorians, he stretched his talent over both the traditional, melodic verse and the less inhibited rhythms of blank verse. In both areas, as previous chapters have illustrated, he had notable successes. Yet in neither area did he develop, in theory or in practice, a prosody which could be relied upon to sustain him through his creative adventures. Unlike a formalist such as Frost, Bryant did not find endless "the possibilities for tune from the dramatic tones of meaning struck across the rigidity of a limited meter."[13] Indeed, his "dramatic tones" have, through the collected works, a discouraging similarity. Nor in blank verse did he always find the pitch and cadence which could keep pace with his intellectual and emotional discoveries. At times during his career —in "Thanatopsis," "The Fountain," and "The Antiquity of Freedom"—his poetic intent coincided with his choice of blank verse, and the promise of a forceful and original voice is made manifest. At other times, however, the long sequence of iambic pentameter lines (which are best read, as Northrup Frye points out, as a four-stress, running rhythm[14]), performed a pedestrian service, doing little to raise prose description and meditation to a level of poetic intensity.

III *The Formal Voice*

Several examples of his formal voice at work can be found among Bryant's experiments in the sonnet form. No established poet in America had, previous to Bryant, been equal to the rigid demands of either the English or Italian variations of the form, and thus Bryant's achievements in this particular area take on a historical and artistic importance. Two sonnets composed in 1824, "Mutation" and "November," indicate the two directions opened up by the poet's concern for form; a third, "To Cole, the Painter, Departing for Europe," illustrates the level of achievement of which Bryant was capable had he persevered in his use of the sonnet.

In "Mutation" Bryant ambitiously adopted an interlocking rhyme scheme in which the fifth and eighth lines of the sonnet pick up the rhyme of the preceding line: ababbcbccdcdee. Yet in spite of the continuity effected by the rhyme, the sonnet breaks into three firm quatrains and a definitive couplet. The initial quatrain argues that grief and remorse are short-lived; the second states that peace inevitably follows pain; and the third quatrain asserts the positive and remedial influence of suffering. Generalizing upon this cycle in the emotional life of man, the concluding couplet urges an acceptance of change or mutation as preferable to "a stable, changeless state." Such a paraphrase is no substitute for the poem, which is reproduced below; but it does serve to point up Bryant's sensitivity to the structure of progressive quatrains, typical of the sonnet form as it had developed in the work of Shakespeare, Milton, and Wordsworth. Also, it may be suggested that the interlocking rhyme scheme in "Mutation," similar in its effect to the *terza rima* in English verse, serves to reinforce through the pattern of sounds the theme of gradual and unceasing "mutation." Bryant employs the iambic pentameter line skillfully to convey the tone of optimistic certitude in the first two quatrains; and, in order to make his couplet sufficiently reflective, he inserts an additional stress to make an iambic hexameter of the fourteenth line.

Nevertheless, the disciplined voice falters, starting at line eight; it has overreached itself. The transition to rhythms of emergent joy is less than successful, in spite of the vigorous emphasis effected by the heavy consonance of lines eight to eleven. The verse strains for its rhymes in lines eleven and twelve, and is nearly overcome by the resultant wordiness and awkwardness. In raising more formal problems than he could successfully handle, Bryant shows, in this poem, both his enterprising nature and his limitations as a poetic craftsman.

MUTATION

They talk of short-lived pleasure—be it so—
    Pain dies as quickly: stern, hard-featured Pain
Expires, and lets her weary prisoner go.
    The fiercest agonies have shortest reign;

And after dreams of horror, comes again
The welcome morning with its rays of peace.
    Oblivion, softly wiping out the stain,
Makes the strong secret pangs of shame to cease:

Remorse is virtue's root; its fair increase
    Are fruits of innocence and blessedness:
Thus joy, o'erborne and bound, doth still release
    His young limbs from the chains that round him press.

Weep not that the world changes—did it keep
A stable, changeless state, 'twere cause indeed to weep.[15]

Less ambitious in its structure and simpler in its progression of mood is the sonnet "November." Although the quatrains contrast with one another and reinforce the Janus-faced quality which the poet imputes to November, the rhymes are simpler and the rhythm is fairly uniform throughout. The elements of the sonnet form, even though they are not fully exploited here, work harmoniously together to define the lyrical response of the poet to the season.

NOVEMBER

Yet one smile more, departing, distant sun!
    One mellow smile through the soft vapory air,
Ere, o'er the frozen earth, the loud winds run,
    Or snows are sifted o'er the meadows bare.
One smile on the brown hills and naked trees,
    And the dark rocks whose summer wreaths are cast,
And the blue gentian-flower, that, in the breeze,
    Nods lonely, of her beauteous race the last.
Yet a few sunny days, in which the bee
    Shall murmur by the hedge that skirts the way,
The cricket chirp upon the russet lea,
    And man delight to linger in thy ray.
Yet one rich smile, and we will try to bear
The piercing winter frost, and winds, and darkened air.[16]

The melodic element prevails in "November," much more than it had in "Mutation." The soothing alliterative effects contribute to the mood and, through their distribution of stress, to the rhythm. By his skillful combination of a restricted meter and rhyme with a pervasive musicality, Bryant was able in the sonnet, in the elegy, and in numerous other regular stanzaic patterns to tap the nonrational and simply emotive sources of his creativity. At those points where he permitted the form itself, either traditional or improvised, to bear the responsibilities of order and coherence, Bryant most fully capitalized upon the virtues of his formal voice. Where euphony was permitted to prevail over meaning, his imagination was least inhibited.

Thus the sonnet "To Cole," which relies principally upon its imagery to convey its meaning, sustains its forceful rhythms and its militant harmonies throughout. The structure is implicit in the poem, modestly hiding its logic in thick folds of sensory experience. The sonnet is simply a reminder, addressed directly to the painter, to view the European scenes which he is about to visit, through the eyes of his early piety, nationalism, and optimism. In observing the picturesque melancholy of cultures eroded by the forces of history—"paths, homes, graves, ruins"— Cole should bear in mind "A living image of our own bright land." Against the imagery of European decay and dissolution, Bryant opposes the vision which Cole had imparted through his huge canvases—of a new world with unsullied open spaces. Without an obtrusive statement to this effect, Bryant draws upon the two accepted denominators of cultivated taste in his day, the "picturesque" and the "sublime," and contrasts them neatly within the limits of the form. One quatrain of exhortation, one quatrain of strident description of the divine wilderness of Cole's canvases, one quatrain of subdued preview of European sights— a thumping heroic couplet restating the exhortation—and a wealth of poetic experience has been condensed into fourteen lines:

TO COLE, THE PAINTER, DEPARTING FOR EUROPE

Thine eyes shall see the light of distant skies;
   Yet, Cole! thy heart shall bear to Europe's strand
   A living image of our own bright land,
Such as upon thy glorious canvas lies;

Lone lakes—savannas where the bison roves—
　Rocks rich with summer garlands—solemn streams—
　Skies, where the desert eagle wheels and screams—
Spring bloom and autumn blaze of boundless groves.

Fair scenes shall greet thee where thou goest—fair,
　But different—everywhere the trace of men,
　Paths, homes, graves, ruins, from the lowest glen
To where life shrinks from the fierce Alpine air—

　Gaze on them, till the tears shall dim thy sight,
　But keep that earlier, wilder image bright.[17]

Similarly, in his use of his classical elegy Bryant relies less upon the structure of ideas than upon the unity imposed by the rhyme and rhythm of the form. In the case of the elegy, the problems are less of rhyme and more of meter; for the basic unit of the eight-foot couplet is easily worked into the conventional quatrain. But the meter of the elegy, as Bryant practiced it, even though the seventh and eighth feet of each couplet asserted a basic iambic pentameter, allowed for considerable substitution in the remaining six feet. For Bryant—who had written in the *North American Review* of 1819 that poetry should avoid "tame iambics" and the "dead waste of dissyllabic feet," and cultivate, instead, "a freer use of trisyllabic feet"[18]— the elegy had the notable advantage of combining a fundamental metrical regularity with a degree of license. Within an elegy, such as "To the Fringed Gentian," Bryant availed himself of his freedom and used effectively both the anapest and spondee without disturbing the smooth movement of the lines. Only two places in "To the Fringed Gentian" reveal Bryant's failure to provide the discipline of the seventh and eighth feet, and both cases can be easily justified by their metrical context. The success of "To the Fringed Gentian" is more than technical, however; and it is the rhythm of temperate despair caught by each successive couplet which combines sound with sense. And it is rhythm, more than thought, which builds the quiet tension through the poem and carefully restrains it until the moment of brief, climactic release—"Blue—blue—. . ."

The melodies of this poem speak for themselves; yet the principle of symmetrical construction, essential to the classical elegy, deserves some comment. Through a combination of alliteration and internal rhyme, Bryant shapes line after line into a delicate unit of the total harmony. Perhaps the principle of balance is obvious in a line such as "Thou waitest late and comest alone," but the equilibrium of "The hour of death draw near to me" is less clear until the repeated consonant sounds—*th, d,* and *r*—are distinguished. And the internal rhyme in the line, "The aged *year* is *near* his end" is also easy to overlook in the anticipation of the end-rhyme. When the occasion demanded, however, Bryant was also capable of constructing an asymmetrical line of great beauty; and it is all the more effective for its bold relief against the surrounding lines. The intricate pattern—formed by the consonants *l, f,* and *t,* and by the vowel sound ōo—contribute to the high point in "To the Fringed Gentian": "B*l*ue—*bl*ue—as if that sky let *fall*/A *f*lower *f*rom its ce*r*u*l*ean wa*ll*."

In spite of its value in leading him to the sensuous and suggestive core of his subject matter, the formal voice, even if perfected, could not fully realize Bryant's total response to his experience. For the demands of form and his own limitations made one thing certain: if he were to cultivate his esthetic sensibility, he must sacrifice those intellectual qualities which he considered to be essential to noble and elevated poetry. His respect for the reasoning faculties of the mind—not, as some might have it, any moral scruples about pleasure—led him into another area of poetic technique where the intellect could have its say. Blank verse had the advantage of scope and permissiveness, and while Bryant was well aware of the fruits of metrical discipline, the very breadth and inclusiveness of his experience demanded a more open form.

IV *Blank Verse*

There are several appropriate ways of considering the technique of his blank verse, but some are obvious and others are blind alleys. To say that Bryant drew from a strong tradition in English poetry—a tradition which runs from Shakespeare, through Milton, and down to Wordsworth—contributes little to our understanding of his motivation or of the spirit in which he adopted this verse form. We know that he was stimulated by Cowper's "The Task" and that the possibilities for combining natural imagery with blank verse were further revealed to him by Thomson's *The Seasons*. But, if books from abroad provided him with certain basic idioms and perhaps with some of his rhythms, such devices tended to be the tools of his art rather than its substance. While Bryant appears to have felt secure in the shadow of precedent, his concern was for personal expression—not for the perpetuation of an art form.

Yet in this direction there is not much to guide us. Bryant offers little criticism, or even unpublished correspondence, that suggests what he felt to be the function of blank verse or its place in his own work. His remarks in the *Lectures,* upon which this discussion must draw, are addressed not to the problems of blank verse but to those of poetry as a whole. This critical silence on an important phase of his work, however, is in itself important. For in this area particularly, Bryant preferred to work intuitively. The meticulous craftsmanship of the elegies and of the sonnets reveals a conscious attention to the details of composition, but the blank verse gives every sign of being written whole and revised diffidently. Even the case which Professor McDowell makes for Bryant's careful reworking of his material hinges largely upon "Thanatopsis"—which he most certainly did labor over—and upon the formal lyrics.[19] In the body of the blank verse there is little to indicate that Bryant did more than polish the more evident rough spots and attend to flaws in organization.

In practice, the voice which speaks out of the blank verse was conditioned by two dominant influences, neither of them, in any strict sense, poetic. The first of these was Bryant's own prose style, a simplified version of the neo-Classical rhetoric. At its worst, the old rhetoric was pedantic, inflated, and intemperate; at its best, it harnessed the forces of wit, logic, and fancy into a well-matched team. In political and religious tracts toward the close of the eighteenth century, this rhetoric strove for an eloquence which would combine rational persuasion with the elevated style of the grand manner. Bryant had pruned from his own prose the more glaring absurdities of the "false sublime," and his career in journalism further encouraged him toward a more direct, honest expression of thought and feeling.[20] Yet the temper of "eloquence" remained, and its assumed relationship between writer and reader was seldom far from Bryant's mind.

Next to this eloquence, the theory of the "association of ideas" was instrumental in molding the blank verse. From this theory, as subsequent discussion will attempt to make clear, Bryant derived both an articulated justification of what impulse led him to do anyway, and a poetic technique for the management of metaphor and symbol. The act of association, as Bryant adapted it to his own purposes, became a vehicle for reflective revery. Conditioned by the experiences of the past and dependent upon the solitude and silence of Nature for its operation, this voice— perhaps best called the "voice of eloquent revery"—would give expression to Bryant's greatest poem, "Thanatopsis," and to the other major works in blank verse: "Inscription for the Entrance to a Wood," "The Prairies," "Monument Mountain," "The Antiquity of Freedom," and "The Fountain."

V *Contributions of Prose Style to the Blank Verse*

The prose style which Bryant formulated and practiced has a distinctive voice that yields no hint of a divided or unrealized self. This voice is fully articulate, consistent, and easily identified. The tone, rhythms, and diction are invariably those of a person of dignity, intellect, and character who speaks to his audience from a slightly elevated podium. In the *Evening Post* and in Bryant's travel accounts and correspondence, as well as in his public addresses, the platform manner is never totally in abeyance. No problems of the relationship of writer to reader obtrude, nor does the attitude of the writer to his materials present any substantial difficulty. Though the voice of reason may lapse from time to time into pathos, it does so because of its high-minded benevolence; if it rises to a pitch of vehement denunciation, it may be understood to do so because of a legitimate indignation; when it strikes a few sparks of wit, the reader recognizes that such levity is an adornment of the educated style.

Whatever the level appropriate to the audience or subject matter, this prose voice had the capacity for bringing a crystalline clarity to diffused ideas and for imposing order upon numerous and sometimes complex materials. The confident and reasonable voice of the editor, traveler, and public speaker imparts its own elevation of purpose and secures dignity to all that it expresses.

This quality of the voice itself—rather than any specific techniques of persuasion, any syntactical formulae, or any ground rules for organizing the prose piece—is what Bryant adopted from the rhetoric learned at school and college. It is a quality which breathes through imagery and rhythm, which pervades the tone of each piece, and which he would use to bring cohesiveness and perspective to the poetry as well as the prose.

In the travel literature, for example, Bryant communicates precisely and selectively; but he suggests little sense of personal involvement with the places seen or with people whom he met. An extreme instance, dated June 19th, 1832, comes from the posthumous *Prose Writings* and tells of his travels through Illinois. During the trip his horse became frightened, "reared and plunged," shook off the saddlebags, then kicked them thoroughly, and ran off, leaving Bryant stranded on the prairie. But in the face of this catastrophe, the writer's style is composed; it almost reaches the point of dead-pan comedy:

> I now thought my expedition at an end, and had the comfortable prospect of returning on foot or of adopting the method called "to ride and tie." I picked up the saddle-bags and their contents, and, giving them to John, I took charge of the umbrellas, which had also fallen off, and walked back for two miles under a hot sun, when I was met by a man riding a horse, which I was very glad to discover was the one that had escaped.[21]

In a tone of similar detachment he tells of crossing Salt Creek and of watching two travelers forced to swim their horses against the current, one of the men being thrown in transit. He describes the squalor and poverty of a family living in a log-cabin on the prairie, and he successfully communicates the experience of lodging there overnight: "The heat of the fire, the stifling atmosphere, the groans and tossings of the sick man, who got up once in fifteen minutes to take medicine or go to the door, the whimperings of the children, and the offensive odors of the place, prevented us from sleeping, and by four o'clock the next morning we had caught and saddled our horses and were on our journey.[22]

Bryant was affected, however, by a few more reactions than gladness and sleeplessness; and a touch of humor graces his dialogue with a Dutch settler, a woman who had provided the travelers with corn bread and milk: "On my saying that I had lived among the Dutch in New York and elsewhere, she remarked that she reckoned that was the reason why I did not talk like a Yankee. I replied that no doubt living among the Dutch had improved my English."[23]

Bryant recognized the limitations of this account—not altogether typical in its dryness of his travel writings—and appended the remark that "What I have thought and felt amid these boundless wastes and awful solitudes I shall reserve for the only form of expression in which it can be properly uttered." Other travel writings—"Letters," as he called them—compensated for their flat recitals of fact with occasional passages describing scenes of pathos or beauty. Thus, in telling of his visit to the Parisian cemetery of Père la Chaise, he remarks especially upon the burial place of the poor: ". . . where those who have dwelt apart from their more fortunate fellow-creatures in life lie apart in death. Here are no walks, no shade of trees, no planted shrubbery, but ridges of raw earth, and tufts of coarse herbage show where the bodies are thrown together under a thin covering of soil. I was about to walk over the spot, but was repelled by the sickening exhalations that rose from it."[24]

Or in his "Letters" telling of a trip to Illinois in 1841, there is this passage—one of several—depicting the natural attractiveness of the countryside: "From the door of one of these dwellings I surveyed a prospect of exceeding beauty. The windings of the river allowed us a sight of its waters and its beautifully diversified banks to a great distance each way, and in one direction a high prairie region was seen above the woods that fringed the course of this river, of a lighter green than they, and touched with the golden light of the setting sun."[25]

Yet always the voice is that of the literate, cosmopolitan gentleman who may observe, note, and express a few pertinent sentiments without fully engaging himself in the flow of life. It is a subjective voice in that the articulate self always remains apart from the experience which it encounters. For all its apparent non-partisan objectivity, it lacks true objectivity—that which respects the integrity and complexity of outward things and which seeks, as the natural scientist seeks, to probe their inner meanings, their causes, and their relationships. This subjective voice, which could speak endlessly of experience as though it were a vast, unrolling panorama, while maintaining its own pedestal unscarred by events, is the voice which speaks also in the blank verse.

Closer to the blank verse in its elevated tone, however, is the language of Bryant's formal orations. The most noted of these were the memorial discourses in which Bryant recounted the lives and assessed the achievements of his deceased contemporaries. Despite the impressionistic vagueness of many of his remarks (Irving, for example, is described as "the best-natured and most amiable of satirists"[26]), Bryant offered to his audiences a wealth of information on lives and works, an impressive accumulation of significant quotations, and a relatively balanced appraisal of men and their works. The carefully directed passages of pathos or irony are generally subordinate to the central tone of sympathetic seriousness. A few metaphors are permitted to appear in order to unite the loosely structured discussion, and in this, as much as in anything, lies the difference between the addresses and the descriptive prose. One such metaphor conveys the ponderous force of a Cooper novel as it slowly develops:

> The progress of the plot, at first, is like that of one of his own vessels of war, slowly, heavily, and even awkwardly working out of a harbour. We are impatient and weary, but when the vessel is once in the open sea, and feels the free breath of heaven in her full sheets, our delight and admiration are all the greater at the grace, the majesty and power with which she divides and bears down the waves, and pursues her course, at will, over the great waste of waters.[27]

Recognizable in this passage are several elements of Bryant's blank verse: the generalized and dignified diction, the rhythms of the parallel constructions building toward a contrived climax, and the closing image of an immense and immortal nature. This voice—which could clothe an acute critical observation in an elocutionary rhetoric and evoke not merely the rational respect due to a work of art but also a true sense of "delight and admiration" as the critic has felt it—was the voice readily adapted to poetry, particularly to that poetry which permitted the platform posturing and the full-chested rhythms of praise and exultation.

VI *Contributions of Associationism to the Blank Verse*

What the prose voice could not provide for the blank verse, however, was the free flow between observation and reflection, between the external events witnessed and recorded and the internal reactions of heart and mind to these events. While the prose voice stood stolidly in the midst of multiple sensations, permitting itself only parenthetical expressions of feeling or thought, the poetic voice was compelled by its own nature to seek fullness of expression even at the risk of disunity.

Bryant had found in his reading in Reid and Stewart, the two leading exponents of the associational movement in British philosophy, an account of how the mind receives and interprets its experiences; but even more important for his poetry was his discovery in Archibald Alison's *Essays on the Nature and Principles of Taste* (1790) of the significant role which the imagination might play.[28] Alison offered to the young poet not only a justification for his reveries but also a prescription for a freer poetry. When Bryant presented the notion of "suggestion" in his *Lectures,* he was not only making a basic point about his own poetry but was also echoing Alison, who had said that "The object itself appears only to serve as a hint, to awaken the imagination and to lead it through every analogous idea that has its place in the memory." When Alison wrote of the succession of ideas which physical objects serve to stimulate as "trains of pleasing and solemn thought arising spontaneously within our minds,"[29] he put the seal of critical approval upon the device used by Bryant in "Thanatopsis," in "Inscription for the Entrance to a Wood," in "The Antiquity of Freedom," and in "The Fountain" whereby the narrator of the poem enters upon the natural scene and—under its influence—lets his mind turn inward upon himself or backward in time.

The advantages of the "association of ideas," in the sense which Alison developed the concept, were clearly those needed by Bryant. He must have been aware, of course, of Wordsworth's successful use of reminiscence in "Tintern Abbey" and other poems, and thus he cannot be considered, even in his early blank verse, as an innovator. But from Alison, and perhaps from Wordsworth, he found a psychological basis upon which he could structure his poems. Neither formal rhyme schemes nor the rhetoric of eloquence could provide him with an intrinsic order, for both were essentially forms of order imposed upon thought and feeling from the outside—from traditional prosody, from the rule books, from the accepted canons of taste. The association of ideas was not, of course, a stream of consciousness, but then respectable poets of the early nineteenth century did not acknowledge the vulgar rumblings of the *id*. They did recognize, however, that there were ineffable truths not touched by the recognized thought of their time, that the reflective process consisted of much more than conditioned responses to beauty as it was visualized centuries before in places thousands of miles away. And while, as an editor, Bryant appreciated the role of language in its argumentative and persuasive capacities, he also understood the human need for forms of order expressive of the autonomous self.

The association of ideas, as Bryant understood it, placed the individual face to face with the simple realities and divine order in Nature and then allowed matters to take their course. The "structure" of the poems was the dynamic structure of the dialogue between man and nature. That the revery generally turned to the past and that the successive images (as in "The Fountain") reveal the history of man from his primitive times were clear indications that Nature's great principle of temporal change was communicated to the poet. That the revery would often bring to light conflicting points of view (as in "The Antiquity of Freedom") was a sign of Nature's transcendence over petty man. That the structure of each of the poems in blank verse develops according to its own particular needs (as in "Thanatopsis" or "Summer Wind") signifies the spontaneous quality of each creative experience and the diversity of forms which the dialogue between man and Nature may take.

If the ideas of association psychology had led Bryant to a more flexible organization for the blank verse, they also brought him to a reconsideration of metaphor and symbol. In a significant passage in the *Lectures* he speaks of "analogies and correspondences" in a manner which anticipates the more sophisticated handling of the problem a decade later in the fourth chapter of Emerson's *Nature*:

Among the most remarkable of the influences of poetry is the exhibition of those analogies and correspondences which it beholds between the things of the moral and of the natural world. I refer to its adorning and illustrating each by the other— infusing a moral sentiment into natural objects, and bringing images of visible beauty and majesty to heighten the effect of moral sentiment. Thus it binds into one all the passages of human life and connects all the varieties of human feeling within the work of creation.[30]

At their worst, these "analogies," as they occur in Bryant's poetry, could be contrived and sentimental. Sometimes they come within the sights of the "pathetic fallacy," for which Ruskin castigated the Romantics. But, at its best, the analogy could be "suggestive" and could break out of the pattern of explicit or stereotyped metaphor. Consistent with the emphasis of Alison, the analogies could rise spontaneously within the poet's mind as his eye rested upon the natural objects appropriate to his solemn and pleasing thoughts.

These analogies were not, of course, limited to the blank verse. "To the Fringed Gentian," "The Death of the Flowers," "To Cole," and "To the Apennines" illustrate how Bryant infused and heightened moral sentiment within the pattern of conventional rhymes. The blank verse, however, in its less restricted outpouring of poetic ideas, carried to a further extreme the binding "into one all the passages of human life." The fine line which generally divides imagery from metaphor becomes gently obscured as all the phenomena of Nature assume the task of suggestion. Observation and reflection, sensuous joy and moral insight blend into one another until the critical task of analysis becomes difficult indeed. A poem like "Monument Mountain" explains itself to some extent, and the analogy between the mountain and human aspiration can be traced through the passages of narration and description. But in "The Prairies" the analogy is less clear, and the prairies suggest a number of relevant ideas with no central thread upon which they can be strung. And in "The Fountain" we are well within the realm of the obscure where meanings lie remote beneath the surface and are fair game only for persevering critics.

VII *"The Painted Cup"*

By way of illustration, a relatively short poem in blank verse, "The Painted Cup," tells us more than a fragment of the better-known poems does. A poem about ways of seeing, it is comparable in its play of perspectives to Wallace Stevens' "Thirteen Ways of Looking at a Blackbird." The infusion of moral sentiment is restrained; the imagery is suggestive within an inclusive framework of meaning. All in all, the poem shows Bryant at his figurative best, for each step in his train of associations contributes to a total perception of this prairie flower.

The first way of seeing is that of the "wanderer": the "dilated eye" through which Bryant himself had first seen the prairies. The vision is pictorial, and each detail is composed within the frame of the vista:

> The fresh savannas of the Sangamon
> Here rise in gentle swells, and the long grass
> Is mixed with rustling hazels. Scarlet tufts
> Are glowing in the green, like the flakes of fire;
> The wanderers of the prairie know them well,
> And call that brilliant flower the Painted Cup.

At this point the strophe breaks and Bryant addresses the reader. He refers to a point made at length in the *Lectures*: the older mythologies are inapplicable within the world revealed by empirical science:

> Now, if thou art a poet, tell me not
> That these bright chalices were tinted thus
> To hold the dew for fairies, when they meet
> On moonlight evenings in the hazel-bowers,
> And dance till they are thirsty. Call not up,
> Amid this fresh and virgin solitude,
> The faded fancies of an elder world. . .

Here the verse, without a break in syntax, launches into the third way of seeing, the empathetic apprehension of the flowers within the natural processes of their environment:

> But leave these scarlet cups to spotted moths
> Of June, and glistening flies, and humming-birds,
> To drink from, when on all these boundless lawns
> The morning sun looks hot. Or let the wind
> O'erturn in sport their ruddy brims, and pour
> A sudden shower upon the strawberry-plant,
> To swell the reddening fruit that even now
> Breathes a slight fragrance from the sunny slope.

Again a shift—another "But"—a relaxing of the strong-stress iambics—and the fourth way of seeing is suggested:

> But thou art of a gayer fancy. Well—
> Let then the gentle Manitou of flowers,
> Lingering amid the bloomy waste he loves,
> Though all his swarthy worshippers are gone—
> Slender and small, his rounded cheek all brown
> And ruddy with the sunshine; let him come
> On summer mornings, when the blossoms wake,
> And part with little hands the spiky grass,
> And touching, with his cherry lips, the edge
> Of these bright beakers, drain the gathered dew.[81]

If mythologies are needed, runs the thought of these closing lines, let them be those of the American aborigines, and let the poet retain the freshness and purity of the primitive imagination.

In "The Painted Cup" Bryant exploited to its fullest the speculative freedom bestowed upon him by the doctrine of the association of ideas. Not only does the use of metaphor and symbol rise above the mechanical comparisons which characterize the lesser poets of any era, but the rhythms themselves, like those of all of his better blank verse, are those of the mind itself as it ponders and meditates. The preponderance of run-on lines, the abundant caesuras, the natural syncopation which occurs when the voice inclines toward a regular pattern of stresses—all of these are the elements which contribute to the rich sonority and high seriousness of Bryant's great works in blank verse. At a further range from the deliberate musicality of the formal lyrics lie the spontaneous rhythms and chance harmonies of these lines. The touches of alliteration, such as those in the line "A sudden shower on a strawberry plant," may contribute to the pervasive sibilance of a passage; elsewhere they may bring an intensification of stress in a particular line, such as "The faded fancies of an elder world"; but the patterns of sound are generally subordinate to the rhythm and to the imagery as they develop through the poem. The blank verse placed a premium on the action of the intellect, and only those sensuous elements which could cooperate with the movement of thought find a place in this verse.

VIII *The Pitfalls of Blank Verse*

If the blank verse drew from these two sources, and was indeed the "voice of eloquent revery," its continued success depended upon a delicate coordination. This is the irony of Bryant's style. While the rhetoric of eloquence could provide him with a stable center for his creative activity, it could also leave his expression vaporous, void of content, and out of touch with his listeners. Though the association of ideas might secure for him the freedom and inwardness that brought his poetry to life, it could easily become a stylistic trick—and one without relevance either to his deeper thoughts or to the eternal truths of Nature. Even in the blank verse of his middle period—"To Earth" (1834), for example—the rhetorical effects could take over and not only leave the language flaccid but also detract from the smooth and suggestive train of ideas. And, as a previous chapter has pointed out, the association of ideas becomes an inert principle once the sense of communion with Nature is lost. Thus, while "Among the Trees" (1868) has many fine lines, its language gradually loses contact with any substantial reality; the poem therefore concludes lamely with a banal figure which might easily have been drawn from an eighteenth-century political tract:

> The hand of ruffian Violence, that now
> Is insolently raised to smite, shall fall
> Unnerved before the calm rebuke of Law,
> And Fraud, his sly confederate, shrink, in shame,
> Back to his covert, and forego his prey.[32]

As a poet, Bryant is no exceptional case; for any creative artist, the pitfalls lie on all sides. If he had bad habits impressed upon him during his back-country education, he made the most of them. If his reading in British literature and philosophy opened up promising new vistas for him, these insights too quickly became mannerisms. Though he developed an extraordinary ear for the musical effects of language early in his career, these very effects militated against the full articulation of his thought. Though he claimed to speak authoritatively for the role of imagination in literature, his aptitude lay not in the creation of startling new effects and prophetic questions but rather in the restatement of old truths and in the resolution of contemporary crises of the heart and mind.

To say that Bryant spoke with a divided voice is an essential criticism, but it need not be a severe one. Along each of the trails that he tramped alone, he left a number of memorable literary landmarks. Nor was his failure absolute, depending as it does upon our assessment of his talent. If we take his best poems, however, as a true index of his ability, he falls short of his own standard of achievement. Unable to assess himself completely as a poet, unwilling to formulate the fast, guiding principles by which his genius would be directed, and uncompromising in his attachment to the two divergent paths along which he was wont to stray, Bryant failed to realize that distinctive originality which is the mark of the great poets of his day and ours.

CHAPTER *6*

"The Dear Old Poet"

A MEMBER of the literary colony summering in the Berkshires in 1850 recalled years later a curious tribute which the group made to a one-time native of the area. The incident, related by James T. Fields, concerned a toast offered during a picnic on a mountain-top. The object of the toast was William Cullen Bryant; among the toasters were Hawthorne, Holmes, Melville, and Duyckinck: ". . . Then we all assembled in a shady spot, and one of the party read to us Bryant's beautiful poem commemorating Monument Mountain. Then we lunched among the rocks, and somebody proposed Bryant's health, and 'long life to the dear old poet.' This was the most popular toast of the day, and it took, I remember, a considerable amount of Heidsieck to do it justice."[1]

Few sophisticated readers will miss the hint of irony which lingers—even for modern ears—in this sentimental adulation of the rising generation for "the dear old poet." Bryant was, first of all, neither "old" relative to the group, nor was he plausibly "dear." On that August day of 1850 he was still vigorously editing the *Evening Post,* he was only fifty-five years of age, and he was merely ten years in advance of Hawthorne himself. As for his being "dear" to any of the group—it seems unlikely. Lowell, in the *Fable for Critics,* was closer to the general view when he caricatured Bryant as an "iceberg."

On the other hand, there is little reason to believe that any deliberate sarcasm was intended. "Monument Mountain" was an appropriate poem for the occasion, and its theme of illicit passion might well have affected the authors of *Pierre* and *The Scarlet Letter.* Bryant is not known to have given offense to any of those present, either as a political writer or as a literary critic. Nor did he, as an artist, pose any serious threat to their literary fortunes. His best-known poems had been published decades before ("Thanatopsis" antedated Herman Melville's birth by two years), and his output during the 1840's presented no serious challenge to anyone. In a sense, he had become a very comfortable institution in American letters—merely a reminder that poetry could flourish in American culture. If Bryant as a man or as an artist was not literally a "dear old poet," he, as a representative man-of-letters, certainly struck the rising generation as being both distantly congenial and also conveniently passé.

I *Reaction*

Bryant symbolized for them, of course, a definite and concluded stage in the progress toward a national literature. Within a very few days of this expedition Melville was to write his famous review of Hawthorne's *Mosses* in which he claimed to have discovered on native ground a genius comparable to that of Shakespeare. Hawthorne, wrote Melville, had the power to "probe to the very axis of reality." Like Shakespeare, he could capture the quality of "blackness" and portray "the sane madness of vital truth."[2]

If Melville's gesture was characteristically grandiose, it still made clear the distinction between the generation of Bryant, Cooper, and Irving and that of Hawthorne, Melville, Poe, Thoreau, and Whitman. In order for the second growth of probers, seekers, and prophets to arise, the old elms had to be transplanted from the creative ground. The new catchwords of "genius," "spirit," "daemonic," and "intuition" in a few years undid the works of lifetimes. The new *Sturm und Drang* could well afford to patronize the less frenzied, less pessimistic, less lyrically irrational artists in whose shade they had been nurtured. The very notion of literary nationalism in America implied a perpetually forward sweep of the creative wave. It was not, after all, the fault of the emergent authors that Bryant had not gracefully removed himself, as Cooper and Irving had done, when his contribution was essentially finished. Yet by patronizing him the same end was accomplished. A few kind critical paragraphs, a jovial toast in Heidsieck, and the shadows of past creative effort were dispelled.

Emerson, Poe, and Whitman each contributed a favorable word or two toward these critical obsequies. Even as early as 1839 Emerson was writing off the entire previous generation, saying that "all the American geniuses . . . Irving, Bryant, Greenough, Everett, Channing, even Webster in his recorded Eloquence, all lack nerve and dagger."[3] Again in 1844 an entry in Emerson's *Journals* identifies Bryant with an era of creativity which had somehow failed: "But in America I grieve to miss the strong black blood of the English race: ours is a pale diluted stream. What a company of brilliant young persons I have seen with so much expectation! the sort is very good, but none is good enough of his sort. Every one an imperfect specimen; respectable, not valid. Irving thin, and Channing thin, and Bryant and Dana; Prescott and Bancroft. . . ."[4]

II *Appreciation*

Yet Emerson was also the most perceptive of readers. He recognized the worth of the poet to the extent of including him on the faculty of an imaginary "ideal" college,[5] and he found solid value in the poems themselves: "Bryant has learned where to hang his titles, namely, by tying his mind to autumn woods, winter mornings, rain, brooks, mountains, evening winds, and wood-birds. Who speaks of these is forced to remember Bryant. [He is] American. Never despaired of the Republic. Dared name a jay and a gentian, crows also. His poetry is sincere."[6]

Thus, once Emerson had vented his lamentations over the state of genius in America, he could come round to an implied acknowledgment of what his generation owed to the previous one. As his quotation illustrates, the debt was three-fold: the love of Nature, loyalty to the democratic way of life, and a rugged integrity. After all, the writer of *Nature, The American Scholar,* and *Self-Reliance* could hardly ignore the very virtues that he had been preaching. Although Emerson might have missed the qualities of intellectual enterprise and imaginative daring in Bryant's poetry, he responded to the purposeful, moral tone. While the creative dialogue of Bryant's nature poems may have been something less than Emerson's "original relation to the universe," still the voice and the posture had much in common. And if Bryant's commonplace language was no match for the charged and fiery eloquence which Emerson and his peers had learned from Edward Everett at Harvard, at least it made occasional contact with the honest vernacular of the people.

While Emerson's praise was genuine enough, he made no gesture toward a rehabilitation of Bryant's reputation by the standards of the mid-century. Poe, on the other hand, seriously worried over the problem of Bryant's "genius." In a review of the *Complete Poetical Works* of 1846, Poe defended those "accuracies and elegancies of style" characteristic of Bryant's poetry, and he maintained that such "artistic skill" was not entirely incompatible with the profounder qualities of soul and mind. Poe asserted, in the face of the prevailing estimate, that "Mr. Bryant has genius, and that of a marked character, but it has been overlooked by modern schools, because deficient in those externals which have become in a measure symbolical of those schools." Yet even in his role as apologist, Poe admitted that "It will never do to claim for Bryant a genius of the loftiest order."[7] For reasons which were never fully developed in his criticism, Poe conceived of at least two distinct ranks of genius, and he generally spoke of Bryant as one comfortably ensconced in the lower rank.

Among Bryant's more sympathetic critics, Whitman was the most extravagant in his praise—and the last to speak out. In a passage from *Specimen Days* titled "My Tribute to Four Poets," he describes the qualities of Bryant's verse in such a way that the unspoken compliment of literary indebtedness is forcefully implied:

> Bryant pulsing the first interior verse—throbs of a mighty world—bard of the river and wood, ever conveying a taste of the open air, with scents as from hay fields, grapes, birch-borders— always lurking fond of threnodies—beginning and ending his long career with chants of death, with here and there through all, poems or passages of poems, touching the highest universal truths, enthusiasms, duties—morals as grim and eternal, if not as stormy and fateful, as anything in Aeschylus.[8]

III *Toward a Modern Appreciation of Bryant*

Thus, even the poet-critics who most deeply responded to Bryant's poetry tended to choke off the channels by which the twentieth-century reader might return to the poems themselves.

Even Whitman's heady praise leads us to the open-shirt bard of Camden rather than to the one who prompted his threnodies. Poe's good-but-not-great equivocation has led much subsequent criticism to award Bryant a dignified post in the second rank.[9] Emerson's approval of his sincerity and pastoral subject matter has kept alive a genteel interest in Bryant's poems, but it has been as successful in later days as it was in the 1840's in precluding active, intelligent curiosity. On the whole, Bryant has in our day been given over to the pedagogues and the researchers. The one side inflicts long passages from "Thanatopsis" upon the startled minds of the young, the other searches for hints of a "usable past" in Bryant's scientism, or patriotism, or liberalism, or whatever other *ism* may be easily detached from the context of the poems.

Yet because Bryant's contemporaries and a few generations of uncritical thought have either missed the key point or have neglected it, we have little excuse, with the corporate sensibility well advanced, to continue in hazardous confusion. The life of poetry has its own integrity. No form of special pleading, no matter how well intentioned, can intervene between the creative voice of the poet and his ultimate audience. If the poem itself has no place in that electric arc of experience, where the charged poles of the individual and his world become proximate, then all peripheral considerations are meaningless also. The poet may speak to the present and lend his grace or wisdom to the enrichment of our lives in a multitude of ways; but he requires of us that we see the world as he saw it and that we share, to the limit of our capacity, those ecstatic and insightful moments recorded in his poems.

Though we no longer demand with the same urgency that the poet speak for "universal" values, the claim of art as it passes down through the years remains the same. The successful lyric poem is still a distillation *and* a crystallization of immediate and personal life. The poet's message is not one of causes or certitudes; it is a promise of visions and values as yet unrealized in ourselves. To ignore the basic enterprise of a poet like Bryant is to lose our own sense of the inestimable importance of art in our lives; and eventually it is to lose our senses of language, form, and beauty as well.

But we do not claim either "genius" or "greatness" for William Cullen Bryant. Let us, as critics and thoughtful readers, leave these matters of prestige and rank to those who find them important. Certainly we can place a high estimate upon his various accomplishments and yet with clear eyes analyze his limitations and his failures. To examine the quandary which we have called his "divided voice" can hardly be taken as a denial that poems in either of his voices—"Thanatopsis" and "To the Fringed Gentian," for example—are triumphs of his art. Nor need we apologize for those aspects of his work which strike us as banal, tendentious, or obscure.

Recognizing the circumstances under which he composed his verse and the standards to which he aspired, we can forgive, and easily forget, the works of lesser significance for us. What we cannot overlook, however, is the noble attempt of the man to forge out of the scraps of an impoverished culture the rails along which men might travel toward a more beautiful and satisfying future. The worst of his poems stand as tokens of expected fulfillment. The best are declarations that the human sensibility can rise independent and vigorous in a new land.

Notes and References

Chapter One

1. "The Poet" (1863; *Thirty Poems*, 1864). The text of this and of most of the poems quoted is that of *The Poetical Works of William Cullen Bryant* (New York, 1876). This final edition of the poems to be compiled during the poet's lifetime has been generally accepted by twentieth-century scholars as the authoritative text. The poems taken from this source will be hereafter noted only by title, by date of composition, and by the place and date of original publication, as above. Poems which did not appear in the edition of 1876 are, however, fully documented in these notes.

2. Parke Godwin, *A Biography of William Cullen Bryant, with Extracts from His Private Correspondence*, in *The Life and Writings of William Cullen Bryant*, I (New York, 1883), 6-28. The influence of the father on the young poet's work is discussed in an article by Donald M. Murray, "Dr. Peter Bryant: Preceptor in Poetry to William Cullen Bryant," *New England Quarterly*, XXXIII (1960), 513-22.

3. *Ibid.*, I, 28-37. See also Tremaine McDowell, "Cullen Bryant at Williams College," *New England Quarterly*, I (1928), 443-66, and *idem*, "William Cullen Bryant and Yale," *New England Quarterly*, III (1930), 706-16.

4. "A Lifetime" (1876; *Collected Poems*, 1876).

5. "Reminiscences of the 'Evening Post,' by William Cullen Bryant" ["Extracted from the *Evening Post* of November 15, 1851, with additions and corrections by the writer."] in John Bigelow, *William Cullen Bryant*, American Men of Letters Series (Boston, 1890), pp. 312-42.

6. Allan Nevins, *The Evening Post: A Century of Journalism* (New York, 1922), p. 350.

7. *Ibid.*, p. 351.

8. "In Memory of William Leggett" (1839; *Democratic Review*, 1839). "In Memory of John Lothrop Motley" (1877; *International Review*, 1877) in *The Poetical Works of William Cullen Bryant*, ed. Parke Godwin, II (New York, 1883), 349. "To Cole, the Painter, Departing for Europe" (1829; *Talisman*, 1830).

9. *The New England Magazine*, 1831, as quoted in Nevins, p. 137.

10. Godwin, *op. cit.*, I, 334.

11. Nathaniel Hawthorne, *Passages from the French and Italian Note-Books* (Boston, 1883), p. 212. Bryant is not identified by name in this passage but the characterization is unmistakable. Bigelow reprints the entire passage (194-96), inserting Bryant's name where the Riverside edition had blanks; but Bigelow dates the meeting in May of 1867, three years after Hawthorne's death.

12. Tremaine McDowell, "Bryant and *The North American Review*," *American Literature*, I (1929), 23.

13. Ralph Waldo Emerson, *Essays*, First Series (Boston, 1890), pp. 282-84.

14. Godwin, *op. cit.*, I, 4, 57-58.

15. *Ibid.*, I, 9.

16. *Ibid.*, I, 77-78. See also Tremaine McDowell, "The Juvenile Verse of William Cullen Bryant," *Studies in Philology*, XXVI (1929), 96-116.

17. *Ibid.*, 114.

18. Godwin, *op. cit.*, I, 27.

19. Tremaine McDowell, *William Cullen Bryant*, American Writers Series (New York, 1935), p. xxv, cites James Grant Wilson, *Bryant and His Friends* (New York, 1885), p. 430, as the source for this information. Articles dealing with Bryant's response to the associational psychology are the following: William Palmer Hudson, "Archibald Alison and William Cullen Bryant," *American Literature*, XII (1940), 59-68; Donald A. Ringe, "Painting as Poem in the Hudson River Aesthetic," *American Quarterly*, XII (1960), 71-83; Charles L. Sanford, "The Concept of the Sublime in the Works of Thomas Cole and William Cullen Bryant, *American Literature*, XXVIII (1957), 434-48. The influence of associational thought in America generally is treated in William Charvat, *Origins of American Critical Theory, 1810-1835* (Philadelphia, 1936). At present the most complete study of Bryant's intellectual development is an unpublished dissertation: Donald A. Ringe, *Poetry and the Cosmos: William Cullen Bryant* (Harvard University, 1953). Although I find myself in disagreement with this work on a number of key issues, it has contributed much to my understanding of Bryant's thought.

20. Godwin, *op. cit.*, I, 33.

21. "To a Waterfowl" (1815; *North American Review,* 1818). For a discussion of the date of composition see William Cullen Bryant II, "The Waterfowl in Retrospect," *New England Quarterly,* XXX (1957), 181-89.

22. *Lectures on Poetry* (April, 1826), first published in *Prose Writings,* ed. Parke Godwin (New York, 1884); reprinted in McDowell, *Bryant,* pp. 184-223.

23. "The Death of Schiller" (1838; *Democratic Review,* 1838).

24. "From the Fifth Book of Homer's Odyssey" (1863; *Atlantic Monthly,* 1865).

Chapter Two

1. Editor's Note, *The Poetical Works of William Cullen Bryant,* ed. Parke Godwin, I (New York, 1883), 351.

2. "The Prairies" (1832; *Knickerbocker Magazine,* 1833). Cf. Ralph N. Miller, "Nationalism in Bryant's 'The Prairies'," *American Literature,* XXI (1949), 227-32.

3. Herman Melville was to underscore these lines in his volume of the *Poems* (New York, 1863): Jay Leyda, *The Melville Log,* II (New York, 1951), 692.

4. "Earth" (1834; New York *Mirror,* 1835).

5. George Arms, "William Cullen Bryant: A Respectable Station on Parnassus," *University of Kansas City Review,* XV (1949), 219-21. My discussion is generally indebted to this article for its concept of "self-dramatization."

6. "The Yellow Violet" (1814; *Poems,* 1821).

7. "To the Fringed Gentian" (1829; *Poems,* 1832).

8. "The Death of the Flowers" (1825; *New York Review,* 1825).

9. "Oh Fairest of the Rural Maids" (1820; *Poems,* 1832).

10. "Monument Mountain" (1824; *United States Literary Gazette,* 1824).

11. "Sella" (1862; *Thirty Poems,* 1864).

12. "The Earth is Full of Thy Riches" (1820), in *Poetical Works,* II (1883), 203.

13. "A Forest Hymn" (1825; *United States Literary Gazette,* 1825).

14. "Inscription For the Entrance to a Wood" (1815; *North American Review,* 1817).

15. "A Summer Ramble" (1826; New York *Mirror,* 1826).

16. "Hymn of the City" (1830; *Christian Examiner,* 1830).
17. "The Old Man's Counsel" (1840; *Democratic Review,* 1840).
18. "Among the Trees" (1868; *Putnam's Magazine,* 1869).
19. "The Order of Nature" (1866; *Poems,* 1871).

Chapter Three

1. "Thanatopsis" (1815-1821; *North American Review,* 1817; *Poems,* 1821). The dating of this poem is discussed subsequently in this chapter.

The basic points regarding Bryant's revision of "Thanatopsis" can be observed in the following text of the poem (from *Poetical Works,* 1876). I have italicized those portions which were added to the main body of the poem subsequent to its original publication in the *North American Review* of 1817. While the opening seventeen lines were not composed until the poet's visit to Cambridge in 1821, the section starting with line 66 had its origins in Manuscript B, c. 1818. For a detailed study of the various texts see Tremaine McDowell, "Bryant's Practice in Composition and Revision," *Publications of the Modern Language Association,* LII (June 1937), 474-502.

THANATOPSIS

To him who in the love of Nature holds
Communion with her visible forms, she speaks
A various langauge; for his gayer hours
She has a voice of gladness, and a smile
And eloquence of beauty, and she glides
Into his darker musings, with a mild
And healing sympathy, that steals away
The sharpness, ere he is aware. When thoughts
Of the last bitter hour come like a blight
Over thy spirit, and sad images
Of the stern agony, and shroud, and pall,
And breathless darkness, and the narrow house,
Make thee to shudder, and grow sick at heart;—
Go forth, under the open sky, and list
To Nature's teachings, while from all around—
Earth and her waters, and the depths of air—
Comes a still voice—Yet a few days, and thee
The all-beholding sun shall see no more
In all his course; nor yet in the cold ground,

Where thy pale form was laid, with many tears,
Nor in the embrace of ocean, shall exist
Thy image. Earth, that nourished thee, shall claim
Thy growth, to be resolved to earth again,
And, lost each human trace, surrendering up
Thine individual being, shalt thou go
To mix for ever with the elements,
To be a brother to the insensible rock
And to the sluggish clod, which the rude swain
Turns with his share, and treads upon. The oak
Shall send his roots abroad, and pierce thy mould.

Yet not to thine eternal resting-place
Shalt thou retire alone, nor couldst thou wish
Couch more magnificent. Thou shalt lie down
With patriarchs of the infant world—with kings,
The powerful of the earth—the wise, the good,
Fair forms, and hoary seers of ages past,
All in one mighty sepulchre. The hills
Rock-ribbed and ancient as the sun,—the vales
Stretching in pensive quietness between;
The venerable woods—rivers that move
In majesty, and the complaining brooks
That make the meadows green; and, poured round all,
Old Ocean's gray and melancholy waste,—
Are but the solemn decorations all
Of the great tomb of man. The golden sun,
The planets, all the infinite host of heaven,
Are shining on the sad abodes of death,
Through the still lapse of ages. All that tread
The globe are but a handful to the tribes
That slumber in its bosom.—Take the wings
Of morning, pierce the Barcan wilderness,
Or lose thyself in the continuous woods
Where rolls the Oregon, and hears no sound,
Save his own dashings—yet the dead are there:
And millions in those solitudes, since first
The flight of years began, have laid them down
In their last sleep—the dead reign there alone.
So shalt thou rest, and what if thou withdraw
In silence from the living, and no friend
Take note of thy departure? All that breathe

Will share thy destiny. The gay will laugh
When thou art gone, the solemn brood of care
Plod on, and each one as before will chase
His favorite phantom; yet all these shall leave
Their mirth and their employments, and shall come
And make their bed with thee. *As the long train*
Of ages glide away, the sons of men,
The youth in life's green spring, and he who goes
In the full strength of years, matron and maid,
The speechless babe, and the gray-headed man—
Shall one by one be gathered to thy side,
By those, who in their turn shall follow them.

So live, that when thy summons comes to join
The innumerable caravan, which moves
To that mysterious realm, where each shall take
His chamber in the silent halls of death,
Thou go not, like the quarry-slave at night,
Scourged to his dungeon, but, sustained and soothed
By an unfaltering trust, approach thy grave,
Like one who wraps the drapery of his couch
About him, and lies down to pleasant dreams.

2. Cf. McDowell, *Bryant*, p. xxv.

3. Godwin, *op. cit.*, I, 37.

4. As quoted in Carl Van Doren, "The Growth of Thanatopsis," *Nation*, CI (1915), 432.

5. Beilby Porteus, "Death, A Poetical Essay," in *A Summary of Christian Evidences* (Boston, 1814), 133-43.

6. McDowell, *Bryant*, p. 350. "Not That From Life and All Its Woes" (1815; *North American Review*, 1817).

7. "Hymn to Death" (1820; *New York Review*, 1825).

8. McDowell, "Bryant's Practice," p. 484.

9. Godwin, *op. cit.*, I, 37.

10. Van Doren, *op. cit.*, p. 432.

11. *Ibid.*, p. 432.

12. McDowell, *Bryant*, p. 353-54. "They Taught Me and It was a Fearful Creed" (c. 1818).

13. Lydia Sigourney, "Versification of a remark by Pliny," *North American Review*, V (1817), 337-38. Also in her volume *Poems; by the Author of Moral Pieces in Prose and Verse* (Boston, 1827).

14. William Cullen Bryant II, "The Genesis of 'Thanatopsis',"
New England Quarterly, XXI (1948), 163-84.

15. Godwin, *op. cit.*, I, 150.

16. McDowell, "Bryant's Practice," pp. 482-84. All references to
the earlier manuscripts are quoted from this source.

17. Cf. Grey's "Ode for Music," "The still small voice of gratitude,"
which is a literal borrowing from I Kings 19:12. Cf. Tennyson, "The
Two Voices," "A still small voice spoke unto me. . . ." The phrase also
has echoes of "The still, sad music of humanity" from Wordsworth's
"Tintern Abbey."

18. Early nineteenth-century sermons by Jedediah Morse and
Lyman Beecher illustrate the perseverance of this form. For further
information upon the structure of the sermon see Perry Miller,
The New England Mind: The Seventeenth Century (Cambridge,
Mass., 1954), pp. 331-51. I first suggested this structural principle
in "Bryant's 'Thanatopsis': A Sermon in Stone," *American Literature*,
XXXI (1960), 474-79.

19. *A Survey of the Summe of Church Discipline* (London, 1648),
Preface, as quoted in Perry Miller and Thomas H. Johnson, *The
Puritans* (New York, 1938), p. 65.

20. Arms, *op. cit.*, pp. 220-22.

21. "The Burial-Place" (1818; *Poems*, 1832).

22. "The Two Graves" (1826; *United States Literary Gazette*,
1826).

23. "Among the Trees" (1868; *Putnam's Magazine*, 1869).

24. "A Lifetime" (1876; *Collected Poems*, 1876).

25. "The Flood of Years" (1876; *Scribner's Monthly*, 1876).

Chapter Four

1. Nevins, *op. cit.*, p. 135.

2. Bigelow, *op. cit.*, p. 341.

3. *Ibid.*, pp. 340-41.

4. *Ibid.*, pp. 341-42.

5. *Ibid.*, p. 234.

6. *The Heart of Emerson's Journals*, ed. Bliss Perry (Boston,
1926), p. 192.

7. Godwin, *op. cit.*, I, 351.

8. Gordon E. Bigelow, *Rhetoric and American Poetry of the
Early National Period*, Univ. of Florida Monographs: Humanities No.
4 (Gainesville, Florida, 1960), pp. 48-59.

9. *The Embargo*, ed. Thomas O. Mabbott (Gainesville, Florida, 1955), pp. 37-48.

10. C. I. Glicksberg, "From the 'Pathetic' to the 'Classical': Bryant's Schooling in the Liberties of Oratory," *American Notes and Queries*, VI (1947), 179-82.

11. Author's Note to "The Ages," quoted from *Poetical Works*, I (1883), 335.

12. "The Ages" (1821; *Poems*, 1821).

13. Godwin, *op. cit.*, I, 171.

14. "The Greek Boy" (1828; *Talisman*, 1829).

15. "The Conjunction of Jupiter and Venus" (1826; *United States Literary Gazette*, 1826).

16. "To the Apennines" (1835; New York *Mirror*, 1835).

17. "The Fountain" (1839; *Democratic Review*, 1839).

18. Donald A. Ringe, "William Cullen Bryant and the Science of Geology," *American Literature*, XXVI (1955), 507-14.

19. *Poetical Works*, I (1883), 354-55.

20. "The Antiquity of Freedom" (1842; *Knickerbocker*, 1842).

21. Godwin, *op. cit.*, II, 188-89.

22. "The Death of Lincoln" (1865).

Chapter Five

1. *Prose Writings*, I, 15. Professor Arms has also pointed out Bryant's "indecisiveness of theory" in his article, *University of Kansas City Review*, XV, 218.

2. *Prose Writings*, I, 7-8.

3. *Prose Writings*, I, 13.

4. McDowell, *Bryant*, pp. lv-lvi. See also Gay W. Allen, *American Prosody* (New York, 1935), pp. 27-55.

5. *A Library of Poetry and Song*, ed. William Cullen Bryant, I (New York, 1875), 47-48.

6. *Library*, I, 48.

7. *Prose Writings*, I, 34.

8. *Library*, I, 47.

9. *Prose Writings*, I, 6.

10. *Ibid.*, I, 6.

11. *Ibid.*, I, 6.

12. "An Essay on American Poetry," *North American Review* (1818), reprinted in *Prose Writings*, I, 45-56.

13. Robert Frost, *Complete Poems* (New York, 1948), p. v.

14. Northrup Frye, *The Anatomy of Criticism* (Princeton, N. J., 1957), p. 251ff.

15. "Mutation" (1824; *United States Literary Gazette*, 1824).

16. "November" (1824; *United States Literary Gazette*, 1824).

17. "To Cole, the Painter, Departing for Europe" (1829; *Talisman*, 1830).

18. *Prose Writings*, I, 57-67.

19. McDowell, "Bryant's Practice," pp. 474-502.

20. Bigelow, *op. cit.*, pp. 72-73.

21. *Prose Writings*, II, 17.

22. *Ibid.*, II, 19.

23. *Ibid.*, II, 21.

24. "Letter I. First Impressions of an American in France," in McDowell, *Bryant*, pp. 264-67.

25. "Letter VII. An Excursion to Rock River," in McDowell, *Bryant*, p. 270.

26. "A Discourse on the Life, Character and Genius of Washington Irving" (delivered April 3, 1860); in *Prose Writings*, I, 332-67.

27. "Discourse on the Life and Genius of Cooper" (delivered Feb. 25, 1852); quoted from *Prose Writings*, I, 329.

28. Archibald Alison, *Essays on the Nature and Principles of Taste* (Edinborough, 1790). See esp., William Palmer Hudson, "Archibald Alison and William Cullen Bryant."

29. Alison, as quoted in Samuel H. Monk, *The Sublime* (Ann Arbor, 1960), pp. 148-49.

30. *Prose Writings*, I, 19.

31. "The Painted Cup" (1842; *Democratic Review*, 1842).

32. "Among the Trees" (1868; *Putnam's Magazine*, 1869).

Chapter Six

1. *Yesterdays with Authors* (Boston, 1878), as quoted in Leyda, I, 384.

2. "Hawthorne and His Mosses," *Literary World* (Aug. 17, 1850), as quoted in Leyda, I, 389.

3. *The Heart of Emerson's Journals,* p. 142.

4. *Journals,* pp. 207-8.

5. *Ibid.,* p. 141.

6. *Ibid.,* pp. 309-10.

7. *Godey's Magazine and Lady's Book,* XXX (April, 1846), as republ. in *Works,* eds. E. C. Stedman and George E. Woodberry, VI (New York, 1914), 134-35.

8. "My Tribute to Four Poets," in *Specimen Days, Complete Prose Works* (New York, 1914), p. 173.

9. See, e.g. McDowell, *Byrant,* p. v; V. L. Parrington, *The Romantic Revolution in America* (New York, 1927), p. 286.

Selected Bibliography

PRIMARY SOURCES

The Embargo. ed. Thomas O. Mabbott. Gainesville, Florida: Scholars' Facsimiles and Reprints, 1955. (Facsimile reprint.)

Letters of a Traveller. New York: G. P. Putnam, 1850.

Letters of a Traveller, Second Series. New York: D. Appleton and Co., 1859.

Letters from the East. New York: G. Putnam and Son, 1869.

The Iliad of Homer. Translated into English Blank Verse. 2 vols. Boston: Fields, Osgood and Co., 1870.

The Odyssey of Homer. 2 vols. Boston: James R. Osgood and Co., 1871-72.

The Poetical Works of William Cullen Bryant. New York: D. Appleton and Co., 1876.

The Poetical Works of William Cullen Bryant. ed. Parke Godwin. 2 vols. New York: D. Appleton and Co., 1883. (Pub. as vols. 3 and 4 of *The Life and Writings of William Cullen Bryant*.)

The Prose Writings of William Cullen Bryant. ed. Parke Godwin. 2 vols. New York: D. Appleton and Co., 1884. (Pub. as vols. 1 and 2 of *The Life and Writings of William Cullen Bryant*.)

SECONDARY SOURCES

ALLEN, GAY W. "William Cullen Bryant." *American Prosody*. New York: American Book Company, 1935. The best published discussion of Bryant's poetic technique.

ARMS, GEORGE. "William Cullen Bryant: A Respectable Station on Parnassus." *University of Kansas City Review*, XV (1949), 215-23. Enlightened, sympathetic appraisal of the poet's major achievements.

BIGELOW, JOHN. *William Cullen Bryant*. American Men of Letters Series. Boston: Houghton, Mifflin Co., 1890. Tame but informed account of his public life.

BRYANT, WILLIAM CULLEN II. "The Genesis of 'Thanatopsis'," *New England Quarterly*, XXI (June, 1948), 163-84. Detailed study refuting traditional assumptions about Bryant's early career.

FOERSTER, NORMAN. *Nature in American Literature*. Boston: The Macmillan Co., 1923. A useful compilation of recurrent images and themes.

GODWIN, PARKE, ed. *A Biography of William Cullen Bryant, with Extracts from His Private Correspondence*. 2 vols. New York: D. Appleton and Co., 1883. Still the best single source for biographical information in spite of omissions and bias.

LEONARD, W. E. "Bryant." *Cambridge History of American Literature*. I. New York: G. P. Putnam's Sons, 1917. Original, penetrating reassessment of the poet and his art.

McDOWELL, TREMAINE. *William Cullen Bryant*. American Writers Series. New York: American Book Co., 1935. Contains a comprehensive, scholarly introduction; representative selections; notes; and a bibliography complete through 1935.

————. "Bryant's Practice in Composition and Revision," *Publications of the Modern Language Association*, LII (June, 1937), 474-502. Thorough study, based upon the original manuscripts, of the early poems.

McLEAN, ALBERT F., JR. "Bryant's 'Thanatopsis': A Sermon in Stone," *American Literature*, XXXI (January, 1960), 474-79.

NEVINS, ALLAN. *The Evening Post: A Century of Journalism*. New York: Boni and Liveright, 1922. Illuminates Bryant's role in journalism and politics.

PARRINGTON, VERNON L. "William Cullen Bryant, Puritan Liberal." *The Romantic Revolution in America*. New York: Harcourt, Brace and Co., 1927. Provocative in interpreting Bryant's political thought; inadequate as literary criticism.

PATTEE, F. L. "The Centenary of Bryant's Poetry." *Sidelights on American Literature*. New York: The Century Co., 1922. Balanced, sensitive criticism of thought and poetry.

PECKHAM, HARRY H. *Gotham Yankee*. New York: Vantage Press, 1950. Modern biography directed toward a popular audience.

QUINN, ARTHUR H. "The Frontiers of Life and Death." *The Literature of the American People*. New York: Appleton-Century-Crofts, 1951. Useful summary of biographical information and criticism.

RINGE, DONALD A. *Poetry and the Cosmos: William Cullen Bryant*. (unpubl. diss.) Harvard University, 1953. Original, thorough study of Bryant's ideas.

Selected Bibliography

————. "Kindred Spirits: Bryant and Cole," *American Quarterly*, VI (Fall, 1954), 233-44. Examines the religious and psychological assumptions underlying nature poetry and landscape painting.

SANFORD, CHARLES L. "The Concept of the Sublime in the Works of Thomas Cole and William Cullen Bryant," *American Literature*, XXVIII (Jan., 1957), 434-48. A stimulating interpretation of romantic aesthetics.

VAN DOREN, CARL. "The Growth of Thanatopsis," *Nation*, CI (1915), 432-33. The first criticism to raise serious questions about this poem.

Index

Index

Index

DATE DUE

AP 30 '72	APR 27 72		
MAY 16 '72	MAY 16 72		
SE 22 '82	MAY 3 '83		
GAYLORD			PRINTED IN U.S.A.